Cooking Basics

Cooking Basics

hamlyn

First published in the U.K. in 1999 by
Hamlyn, a division of Octopus Publishing Group Limited
2–4 Heron Quays, London E14 4JP

Reprinted 2001

Copyright © 1999, 2001 Octopus Publishing Group Limited

ISBN 0 600 60607 4

Printed in Hong Kong

NOTES
Both metric and imperial measurements have been given in all recipes. Use one set of measurements only, and not a mixture of both.

Standard level spoon measurements are used in all recipes.
1 tablespoon = one 15 ml spoon
1 teaspoon = one 5 ml spoon

Eggs should be medium to large unless otherwise stated.
The Department of Health advises that eggs should not be consumed raw. This book contains dishes made with raw or lightly cooked eggs. It is prudent for more vulnerable people, such as pregnant and nursing mothers, invalids, the elderly, babies and young children, to avoid uncooked or lightly cooked dishes made with eggs. Once prepared, these dishes should be kept refrigerated and used promptly.

Meat and poultry should be cooked thoroughly. To test if poultry is cooked, pierce the flesh through the thickest part with a skewer or fork — the juices should run clear, never pink or red. Do not re-freeze poultry that has been frozen previously and thawed.
Do not re-freeze a cooked dish that has been frozen previously.

Milk should be full fat unless otherwise stated.

Nut and Nut Derivatives
This book includes dishes made with nuts and nut derivatives. It is advisable for customers with known allergic reactions to nuts and nut derivatives and those who may be potentially vulnerable to these allergies, such as pregnant and nursing mothers, invalids, the elderly, babies and children, to avoid dishes made with nuts and nut oils. It is also prudent to check the labels of pre-prepared ingredients for the possible inclusion of nut derivatives.

Pepper should be freshly ground black pepper unless otherwise stated.

Fresh herbs should be used, unless otherwise stated. If unavailable, use dried herbs as an alternative, but halve the quantities stated.

Measurements for canned food have been given as a standard metric equivalent.

Ovens should be pre-heated to the specified temperature — if using a fan-assisted oven, follow the manufacturer's instructions for adjusting the time and the temperature.

Vegetarians should look for the 'V' symbol on a cheese to ensure it is made with vegetarian rennet. There are vegetarian forms of Parmesan, feta, Cheddar, Cheshire, Red Leicester, dolcelatte and many goats' cheeses, among others.

Contents

Introduction

'Cooking becomes a fun and fulfilling activity when you feel confident and able enough to experiment. ...'

Successful cooking is within easy reach of everyone, if you know where to start and take the right approach. This means getting to know the basic principles that will provide a solid framework on which to build your developing cookery skills and experience.

But learning the basics does not mean laboriously following lengthy and complicated methods. In contemporary cooking, the emphasis is on simplicity, speed and tastebud-appeal rather than on fancy culinary devices. This opens up the opportunity to cook with freedom, following your individual choice of ingredients and flavourings, without fear of doing things the wrong way. Cooking becomes a fun and fulfilling activity when you feel confident and able enough to experiment. From that moment on, you will never look back!

Getting Organised

Before you begin to cook in earnest, take a long, hard look at your kitchen and see how you can organise and free-up the existing space so that you have as much clear work surface at your disposal as possible. Make sure that you have enough cupboard space available at close hand to stock up on staples, such as dried pasta, rice, dried fruit, canned foods, such as tomatoes and beans, and a range of dried herbs and spices. You will soon get to know which ingredients you use the most.

The following pages offer you guidance on the most useful tools and utensils for your day-to-day cooking requirements. Only buy more specialised items of equipment as and when the need arises.

Cooking with Confidence

Confidence is really the key to preparing good food, and *Get Cooking!* is organised in such a way as to encourage you to extend your culinary expertise step by easy step. Each chapter focuses in turn on a basic ingredient or group of ingredients, or area of cooking, such as desserts and puddings, and cakes and biscuits. Starting with a chapter on eggs, for example, the text gives you straightforward instructions on how to poach, boil, fry, scramble and bake eggs, as well as exactly how to cook the perfect omelette. The chapter goes on to cover making pancakes and batter puddings, including basic recipes, together with interesting serving ideas.

Practical and Versatile

This sets the pattern for the rest of the book, giving you information on choosing and using every kind of ingredient, including advice on storage and preparation, and following on with fail-safe versions of standard recipes. Where appropriate, the book also offers short-cut options, to save on time and energy, and tips for avoiding pitfalls or rescuing mistakes. For maximum versatility and personal choice, the book also includes variations on the basic recipes, together with suggestions for different flavour combinations to try.

Updated and 'New' Classics

Besides presenting the preparation and cooking techniques you need to tackle any recipe, alongside the core recipes of modern-day cookery, each chapter gives you a selection of recipes that employs or builds on those basic skills. Here, you will find classic recipes drawn from the popular cuisines of the world that have stood the test of time and changing food fashions, often with a contemporary twist. In addition, it features some of the 'new classics' – inspiring dishes that bring together ingredients in imaginative combinations.

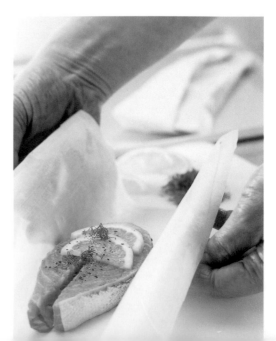

' ... From that moment on, you will never look back!'

Everyday Meals and Entertaining

While many of the dishes included in the book are for everyday eating, there are definitive recipes for those major culinary challenges, for example, the Christmas centrepiece meal and a celebration cake to mark that all-important special family occasion. Other recipes have been specially chosen for their ability to impress while being deceptively easy to prepare, to take the tension out of entertaining.

Your Kitchen Companion

All in all, *Get Cooking!* offers everything you need in one volume to create great dishes right from the word go. Use it as your practical, everyday adviser in the kitchen, as well as a source of inspiration for your cooking. You will derive great pleasure not only from sampling the results of your labours but from the satisfaction of having produced something well. So, with no more ado, get cooking!

Tools of the trade

To cook successfully, you need to invest in a basic range of good-quality tools and utensils. This need not be extensive, but a collection of well-chosen items are essential to achieve the best results as well as to save on unnecessary effort and time.

Knives

A good set of knives should come top of your list of priorities. It is worth getting a well-made set of stainless steel or carbon steel, forged in one piece with a riveted wooden or plastic handle. They should be sharpened regularly and kept separately in a wooden block or on a magnetic rack, rather than in a drawer with other implements, to avoid dulling or damaging the blades.

Chopping Knife: A heavy wide-bladed knife is ideal for chopping vegetables, herbs and other ingredients. It is also useful for transferring chopped ingredients from the chopping board to the cooking pan. The side of the blade can also be used for crushing garlic (see page 143).
General Kitchen Knife: A medium-sized all-

purpose knife – usually about 15–25 cm/6–10 inches long – which can be used for chopping, slicing and cutting all kinds of ingredients.
Paring Knife: This small knife is ideal for trimming and peeling fruit and vegetables.
Bread Knife: A large knife with a serrated edge is useful for slicing bread, cakes and pastries, since it does not tear the food.

Vegetable Peeler

In addition to its usual function, ie removing the skin from vegetables and fruit, a vegetable peeler can be used in more creative ways, for example to pare carrot and courgette ribbons (see page 142), or to make quick and easy chocolate curls (see page 243) or Parmesan cheese curls for use in salads and to garnish other savoury dishes.

Garlic Press

This useful tool finely crushes garlic cloves by forcing the unpeeled flesh through a series of tiny holes. This releases the oils and therefore the full flavour of the garlic into the dish. It also saves your hands from coming into contact with the garlic juices and their pungent aroma lingering on the skin.

Grater

Multi-purpose graters come in a box shape or a single flat sheet. They have different perforations for preparing various kinds of ingredients. The fine holes are used for grating whole spices and citrus rind; the medium and large holes are for grating fresh root ginger, cheese and vegetables. There is a special miniature grater for grating whole nutmegs (see page 196), but either of the ordinary varieties of grater can be used instead.

Masher

A useful tool for mashing potatoes and other root vegetables, such as swede and parsnips.

Balloon Whisk

This is used to blend ingredients, such as butter and flour in sauces, for whisking egg whites and cream and to incorporate air into batter mixtures.

Rolling Pin

An essential item for rolling out pastry and also pasta and bread doughs. Rolling pins are available with or without handles and made out of wood, plastic, nylon or marble.

Paster Server

A useful long-handled stainless steel spoon designed to transfer pasta or noodles from the cooking pan onto a serving dish. It has teeth that grasp the pasta and a hole that allows the cooking liquid to drain back into the pan.

Tongs

These are handy for picking up items of hot food or for turning them when grilling or barbecuing.

Two-pronged Fork

A metal fork with two long prongs will hold meat firmly while it is being lifted from a roasting pan or casserole.

Wooden Spatula

This has a wide, blunt blade and is useful for moving ingredients around in a pan or bowl. For instance, when cooking an omelette, it can be used for drawing the egg mixture into the centre of the pan and for folding the omelette over. Being wooden, it will not scratch pans, nor will the handle burn your hand.

Turner

A turner, or fish slice, is an indispensable tool for lifting and turning all kinds of food, such as rashers of bacon, fried eggs or pieces of meat or fillets of fish.

Palette Knife

Consisting of a long, flexible round-ended metal blade set in a handle, a palette knife is essential for spreading and smoothing the surface of cake mixtures and icings, and useful for scraping mixtures from around the inside of a bowl. It is also useful for lifting up and flipping over pancakes (see pages 18–19)

Perforated Spoon

A large spoon with perforations which is useful for lifting food from a pan, reserving the cooking oil or liquid.

Tenderiser

A tenderiser is a type of wooden mallet with teeth – either wooden or metal – on the underside of the head. This is used to beat cuts of meat in order to break down the connective tissue that makes it tough.

Pestle and Mortar

A grinder and a bowl respectively, this is used for grinding herbs, for example for pesto (see page 37), and whole spices. It can be made of marble, which does not absorb flavours, wood or ceramic.

Cheese Slicer

A simple yet effective tool for cutting thin, even slices from a block of hard cheese.

Pizza/Pasta Cutter

This is a useful implement for cutting pizzas for serving, or for cutting pastry and home-made pasta dough during preparation. Choose a type of cutter that has a guard to protect your fingers, and check that the wheel turns freely.

Sieve

A fine-mesh stainless steel sieve is essential for sifting and straining. It can also be used for puréeing, by rubbing vegetables, pulses or fruit through the mesh with the back of a ladle or wooden spoon.

Mixing Bowl

Choose one made from heatproof glass or ceramic, which will be heavy enough to sit firmly on the work surface. It should also be large and wide enough to enable mixtures to be vigorously whisked or beaten without spilling over the rim.

Chopping Boards

It is best to have two chopping boards – one wooden which you can use for most tasks and the other made from a non-porous material to be kept solely for the preparation of meat and poultry, to avoid contamination

Saucepans

It is wise to invest in a set of good-quality, stainless steel saucepans that will last for years to come. These should be well-balanced and easy to hold, as well as having welded handles and lids that fit tightly. You will need about 3–4 saucepans in the range of 1–7 litres/1¾–12 pints.

Frying Pan

The best type of frying pan is made of heavy gauge, heat-conducting metal, which allows heat to be transmitted rapidly and evenly. It should have a wide, flat base and shallow sides, sloping outwards to give space for lifting and turning food. A long handle makes it easier to lift.

Colander

Choose a colander made from stainless steel with a long handle and a stable base, so that it can be held firmly while draining pasta or vegetables. It can also be used to steam food in place of a proper steamer.

Steamer

This consists of a perforated container, which holds foods to be steamed, inside a pan with a tight-fitting lid, which contains boiling water. Steaming food is an excellent cooking method for maintaining the maximum texture and flavour of foods, while avoiding the use of cooking oils or fats.

Baking Tins

Some baking tins have bright, shiny surfaces that deflect the heat away from the contents so that they do not scorch, while others have dark finishes that absorb and hold the heat. Tin plate is most widely used for bakeware. Aluminium, a good conductor of heat, is more expensive than tin.

Non-stick surfaces, applied to either tin or aluminium, are hard-wearing but can easily be damaged by metal implements.

Choose tins that are sturdy, smooth inside with no crevices for trapping food and with rolled edges which will make them easier and safer to handle.

Cake Tins: The most useful of these is a 20 cm/8 inch or 23 cm/9 inch round tin – a 20 cm/8 inch square tin is the equivalent capacity of a 23 cm/9 inch round tin – and two 20 cm/8 inch round sandwich tins.
Flan Tins: These can be used for sponges or pies. Some have fluted edges and there is a choice between removable and fixed-base varieties. Flan tins are preferable to porcelain flan dishes, since they conduct heat effectively which prevents soggy pastry.
Patty Tin: This is a sheet of cup-shaped hollows for baking tartlets, small cakes or individual Yorkshire puddings.
Loaf Tin: A 1 kg/2 lb loaf tin is very useful for baking bread and tea breads as well as for cooking pâtés.

Pie Dish

For cooking sweet and savoury pies, a classic pie dish is oval-shaped with sloping sides and a wide, flat rim for holding the pastry lid and a capacity of 1.2 litres/2 pints. A pie plate is shallower and usually round.

Measuring Jug

This is a standardised measure with a pouring lip. It is usually marked in both metric and imperial. Available in a variety of materials, the most useful is made from *Pyrex*, which will withstand boiling liquids and you can see very clearly exactly how much is in the jug. Because it is a poor conductor of heat, the handle remains cool.

Eggs

How to Cook Eggs

Choosing and Storing Eggs

Eggs are sold by size graded into very large, large, medium and small. As a general rule, choose large eggs for recipes. Very large and large are a good choice for boiling, frying, poaching, scrambling and omelettes, and small are useful for binding ingredients or glazing. Fresh eggs keep for about 2 weeks. Cool storage is essential to keep eggs fresh, but remember to remove them from the refrigerator 20–30 minutes before use.

Testing Eggs for Freshness

Very fresh eggs are best for poaching and whisking, and are also easier to separate. Egg shells are porous, allowing moisture to evaporate from the white and air to enter, forming a pocket between the shell and the lining membrane. The older eggs are, the larger the air pocket at the rounded end of the shell. This acts as a float, so this quick test can be used to indicate the freshness of an egg.

Dissolve 1 tablespoon salt in 600 ml/1 pint water and lower the egg into it. A very fresh egg will sink and lie on its side. If it lies at a slight angle it is about a week old and if it tilts straight upwards or floats it is stale.

Another test is to break the egg on to a plate. If the egg is fresh, the yolk will stand clearly above the white, as a plump dome, and the white will have two distinct layers: around the yolk it will be thick and gelatinous, with a distinctly thinner outer layer. A stale egg has a flatter yolk, with less distinction between the two layers of egg white.

Poaching Eggs

A perfect poached egg is lightly set and compact in shape. You will need very fresh eggs to achieve this. Pour about 4 cm/ 1½ inches water into a frying pan and add a little salt. Put the pan over a low heat and bring the water just to simmering point – too

many bubbles will cause the egg white to break up before it sets. Break the egg into a cup or small dish and slide it into the water. If necessary, gently stir the water around the egg to draw the white into shape. Leave to poach over a very low heat for 2–3 minutes, until the white is just set, but the yolk is still soft.

Boiling Eggs

Eggs may crack if plunged straight into boiling water, especially if they are cold. To avoid this, carefully prick the rounded end with a pin before cooking. If the shell does crack, sprinkle a little salt on the crack to help the white set.

Method 1 – Using Cold Water

Place the eggs in a saucepan and pour in enough cold water to cover them completely. Place over a high heat. As soon as the water reaches boiling point, reduce the heat so that the water simmers and time the cooking.

Cooking times for eggs (large):

Soft boiled eggs	3–4 minutes
Firm white, runny yolk	4 minutes
Hard-boiled eggs	10 minutes

Method 2 – Using Hot Water

Lower the eggs into a pan of simmering water to cover them completely. Bring back to simmering point and time the cooking.

Cooking times for eggs (large):

Soft boiled eggs	3–4 minutes
Firm white, runny yolk	7 minutes
Hard-boiled eggs	12 minutes

TIP • To prevent hard-boiled eggs overcooking and avoid the formation of a black ring around the yolk, drain them immediately at the end of cooking. Tap on a hard surface to crack the shell, then leave the eggs in cold water to cool.

3

Frying Eggs

Heat about 2 teaspoons oil or melted bacon fat in a heavy or non-stick frying pan until really hot. Break an egg into a cup and quickly tip it into the pan – the white should begin to set immediately. Reduce the heat to medium and spoon the fat over the egg to cook the top surface. Cook for about 1 minute or until the white is set. Use a fish slice to lift the egg from the pan and drain on absorbent kitchen paper.

Making Scrambled Eggs

Beat the eggs with a fork, adding salt and pepper to taste. Add 1 tablespoon milk for every 2 eggs if you like a creamy mixture. Melt 15 g /½ oz butter in a heavy or non-stick saucepan and add the eggs, then stir gently over a medium heat until they are beginning to set. Grated cheese, strips of smoked salmon, diced cooked bacon or snipped fresh chives can be added to the basic mixture.

Baking Eggs

Baked *en Cocotte*

For each egg, put a small knob of butter in a ramekin dish and place in a preheated oven, 160°C/325°F/Gas Mark 3, until melted. Break 1 egg into each dish. Sprinkle with salt and pepper and bake for 10 minutes or until set.

Making a Classic Omelette

1 For each omelette to serve 1 person, break 2–3 eggs into a bowl and beat lightly with a fork, just enough to break up the egg. Add salt and pepper and 1 tablespoon water.
2 Heat a small knob of butter in an 18 cm/ 7 inch omelette pan or small frying pan until it is foaming, but not browned.

3 Pour in the eggs and leave for a few seconds until they begin to set around the edge. Use a spatula or fork to draw the sides of the egg towards the centre, so that the liquid egg flows to the edge.
4 When most of the egg is set, spoon the chosen filling over the middle of the omelette. Alternatively, fold the omelette if it is to be served plain. Use a spatula or palette knife to fold one side over to enclose the filling as you roll the omelette over from the pan on to the plate.

VARIATIONS • Add 1 tablespoon mixed chopped chives, parsley and tarragon to the beaten eggs, or sprinkle 25 g/1 oz grated Gruyère or Cheddar cheese over the omelette before folding it.

4

Vegetable Frittata

A frittata is a substantial kind of omelette in which the eggs and 'filling' are mixed together in the pan, rather than cooked separately. It may then be cooked under the grill or, as here, in the oven.

Serves: **4–6**

Preparation time: 5 minutes

Cooking time: 25 minutes

Oven temperature: 200°C/400°F/Gas Mark 6

2 tablespoons olive oil
2 onions, finely sliced
2 garlic cloves, crushed and chopped
2 potatoes, boiled and sliced
2 red peppers, cored, deseeded and cut into
  strips
6 courgettes, sliced
1 thyme sprig, chopped
5 eggs, lightly beaten
50 g/2 oz Parmesan cheese, freshly grated
salt and pepper
mixed-leaf salad, to serve (optional)

1 Heat the olive oil in a frying pan with an ovenproof handle or a shallow flameproof casserole. Add the onions, garlic, potatoes, red peppers and courgettes and sauté for 5 minutes.

2 Add the thyme, season with salt and pepper to taste and mix well. Pour in the beaten eggs and cook over a moderate heat for 3 minutes.

3 Sprinkle with the grated Parmesan and put the pan or casserole in a preheated oven, 200°C/400°F/Gas Mark 6, and cook for 15 minutes. The frittata should be set and golden on top.

4 Remove the pan from the oven, ease a palette knife all the way around the edge and under the frittata, slide it on to a large plate and serve at once. Serve with a mixed-leaf salad, if liked.

VARIATION • You could substitute 4 shallots for the onions and 1 diced large aubergine for the potatoes. Other suitable cheeses include Cheddar, Gouda and Gruyère.

Making Batters

Batters have many different uses. They are used for pancakes and sweet or savoury puddings as well as for coating a variety of foods for frying. The thickness of the batter depends on its particular use and on the individual recipe.

Basic Pancake Batter

Makes: **8**
Preparation time: 10 minutes
Cooking time: about 15 minutes

125 g/4 oz plain flour
pinch of salt
1 egg, beaten
300 ml/½ pint milk or half milk and half water

Place the flour and salt in a mixing bowl and make a well in the centre. Add the egg to the well in the dry ingredients. Gradually stir in half the milk or milk and water, then beat thoroughly until the batter is smooth and lump-free. Gradually beat in the remaining liquid until the surface is covered in tiny bubbles. Chill the batter for at least 30 minutes before using.

Making Perfect Pancakes

1 Make a pancake batter about 30 minutes before you need it, and keep in the refrigerator until ready for use.
2 Grease a special heavy-based, shallow pancake pan or 18 cm/7 inch frying pan with oil.

Heat a small knob of butter in the pan until it is foaming but not browned.
3 Pour in a little batter, tilting and turning the pan so that the batter coats the surface thinly and evenly.
4 Reduce the heat to moderate and cook until the underside of the pancake is golden brown.
5 Loosen the pancake around the edge with a palette knife, then turn it over, either by tossing it with a quick flick of the wrist or by flipping it over with the palette knife.
6 Cook the other side until golden brown, then turn the pancake out on to a plate. Cover with a piece of non-stick baking paper so that the next pancake can be stacked on top. Continue until all the batter is used.

3

Making Light Yorkshire Puddings

You will need 12 deep muffin tins. Pour ½ teaspoon oil into each tin and place in a preheated oven, 220°C/425°F/Gas Mark 7, for about 5 minutes or until very hot. Quickly pour the batter in to the tins to half-fill and return them to the oven. Bake for about 20 minutes until well-risen, crisp and golden brown.

Making Fruit Popovers

Add 1 tablespoon caster sugar and 1 teaspoon vanilla essence to the batter. Drop banana or apple slices, or soft fruits, such as strawberries or blueberries, into the batter-filled muffin tins just before baking.

Basic Coating Batter

Makes: about 250 ml/8 fl oz
Preparation time: 5 minutes

60 g/2½ oz self-raising flour
60 g/2½ oz cornflour
pinch of salt
1 tablespoon sunflower oil
150 ml/¼ pint milk or half milk and half water
1 egg white

Sift the flour, cornflour and salt into a large bowl and make a well in the centre. Add the oil and milk or milk and water, then beat until smooth and bubbly. In a clean bowl, whisk the egg white in a clean bowl until it holds soft peaks, then fold it quickly into the batter. Use the batter for coating foods such as fish fillets, apple rings, or vegetable chunks, and deep-fry in hot oil, 180°C/350°F, until crisp and golden.

VARIATIONS • For a really crisp, light batter, use beer instead of the milk or milk and water. This beer batter is ideal for coating fish, prawns or vegetables.

Serving Ideas for Pancakes

Rolling

Traditional sweet pancakes are usually sprinkled with sugar and freshly squeezed lemon juice, and rolled up. To do this easily, tuck the edge of the pancake between the prongs of a fork and twist the fork around.

Making Fans

Fold the cooked pancake in half, then fold it again into quarters, to make a fan shape. Spoon filling between the layers of pancake.

Making Crêpe Baskets

Stand a number of small ovenproof bowls (one for each pancake) upside down on a baking sheet. Preheat the oven to 200°C/400°F/Gas Mark 6. Drape the cooked pancakes over the bowls and bake for about 10 minutes, until set into shape. Carefully lift the crêpe baskets off the bowls and fill with fruit, ice cream or a savoury mixture.

Basic Pudding Batter

Makes: about 400 ml/14 fl oz
Preparation time: about 10 minutes

125 g/4 oz plain flour
pinch of salt
2 eggs
150 ml /¼ pint milk or half milk and half water

Make the batter as for the Basic Pancake Batter on page 18.

Spinach Pancakes

Spinach and cheese is a classic combination, used here to fill savoury pancakes. You can use any of your favourite cheeses in this easy recipe.

Makes: **8**

Preparation time: 15 minutes

Cooking time: 15–20 minutes

BATTER
125 g/4 oz plain flour
½ teaspoon salt
1 egg
300 ml/½ pint milk
1 tablespoon vegetable oil
butter, for greasing
FILLING
250 g/8 oz frozen spinach, thawed
125 g/4 oz grated Cheddar cheese

1 Make the batter using the first 4 ingredients and following the method on page 18. Lightly oil a 15 cm/6 inch omelette pan and cook 8 pancakes. Lightly grease a flameproof dish.

2 To make the filling, cook the spinach according to the packet instructions. Drain thoroughly, squeezing out as much liquid as possible and then chop finely.

3 Add half the grated cheese to the spinach mix well and keep warm.

4 Divide the spinach mixture between the pancakes, and roll them up. Place the pancakes in the prepared dish, sprinkle with the remaining cheese and grill quickly to brown. Serve hot.

Using Egg Whites

Separating Eggs

Many recipes require only the white of an egg, or yolk. It is important to separate eggs cleanly. For example, even a trace of yolk can prevent an egg white becoming stiff when whisked.

Tap the egg against the rim of a bowl to crack it around the middle. Holding the egg over the bowl, carefully open the shell with your thumbs, holding the two halves together to let some of the white run out. Gently tip the yolk from one half of the shell to the other, letting the white run into the bowl and taking care not to break the yolk. If you are separating more than 1 egg, use a second bowl and tip the whites into the main bowl when separated, just in case a yolk should break and spoil the whole batch of whites.

Whisking Egg Whites

A large balloon whisk is the best tool to use, since it incorporates as much air as possible

into the whites. However, an electric hand mixer will also give good results if preferred. Choose a large, wide bowl to allow plenty of air to be whisked in.

Before you start, make absolutely sure that the bowl and whisk are completely clean and grease-free, since any trace of grease will give the whisked whites a poor volume, and you may find they will not whisk stiffly at all.

Begin whisking slowly until the egg whites are broken up and bubbles appear. Then continue to whisk hard and fast until the egg whites begin to hold their shape. Try lifting the whisk from the mixture – at first the whites will hold soft peaks, bending over slightly at the peak. If you continue to whisk, the foam will become stiffer and as you lift the whisk the peaks will form stiff points which stay firm and upright. Depending on the recipe, whisk the whites to soft or stiff peaks, but take care not to overwhisk. Overwhisked whites become dry and powdery, and it is difficult to fold them into mixtures. Use the whisked whites straight away: if they are left to stand, the foam will begin to collapse and it cannot be re-whisked.

Folding In Egg Whites

It is important that the mixture into which you are folding whisked egg whites is neither too hot nor too cold, since either can cause much of the volume to be lost. First lighten the mixture by stirring in 1–2 tablespoons of the whisked whites – this makes it easier to fold in the rest without knocking out too much air. Use a large metal spoon to fold in the whites lightly, with a cutting and folding action, until the mixture is evenly mixed, with no white clumps of foam remaining.

Perfect Meringues

A classic meringue 'suisse' is white and crisp, light and sweet. To achieve this you will need very stiffly whisked egg whites and a low heat to dry the mixture out slowly, without browning the meringues.

Serves: **6**
Preparation time: about 20 minutes
Cooking time: 2–3 hours
Oven temperature: 110°C/225°F/Gas Mark ¼

3 large egg whites
175 g/6 oz caster sugar

1 Line a baking sheet with non-stick baking paper. Whisk the whites in a large bowl until they form stiff peaks.
2 Gradually whisk in about half the sugar, a tablespoonful at a time, whisking hard between each addition, until the meringue is very stiff.
3 Fold in the rest of the sugar lightly and evenly using a large metal spoon.
4 Spoon or pipe the mixture into about 12–14 rounds or ovals on to the baking sheet, then place in a preheated oven, 110°C /225°F/Gas Mark ¼ for 2–3 hours, until the meringues are crisp and dry but still white.
5 Carefully lift the meringues from the paper and cool on a wire rack. Sandwich the meringues together with whipped cream or crème fraîche, and serve with summer fruits or chocolate sauce.

Tips for Perfect Hot Soufflés

1 Preheat the oven thoroughly before you start, so that it is at the right temperature when the soufflé goes in.
2 Put the soufflé dish on a baking sheet so that it is easy to lift in and out of the oven.
3 Fill no more than three-quarters full.
4 Serve the soufflé immediately it is cooked.

Layered Cheese and Tomato Soufflé

A soufflé never fails to impress although it is, in fact, astonishingly easy to make. It is important the soufflé is served immediately it is ready, otherwise it will collapse disappointingly.

Serves: **4**

Preparation time: 15 minutes, plus cooling

Cooking time: 45–60 minutes

Oven temperature: 190°C/375°F/Gas Mark 5

25 g/1 oz butter, plus extra for greasing
1 garlic clove, crushed
1 small onion, chopped
375 g/12 oz tomatoes, skinned and chopped
2 teaspoons dried oregano
6–8 black olives, pitted and chopped
salt and pepper
SOUFFLÉ MIXTURE
40 g/1½ oz butter
40 g/½ oz plain flour
300 ml/½ pint single cream or milk
3 large eggs, separated
150 g/5 oz full-fat soft cheese with garlic and
  herbs, crumbled

1 Melt the butter in a heavy-based saucepan. Add the garlic, onion and tomatoes and fry over a low heat, stirring occasionally, for 3–4 minutes. Add the oregano and olives and season with salt and pepper to taste. Remove the pan from the heat and set aside to cool.

2 Meanwhile, make the soufflé. Melt the butter in a saucepan. Add the flour and cook, stirring constantly for 1 minute. Remove the pan from the heat and gradually add the cream or milk, stirring vigorously after each addition to ensure that it is fully incorporated. Return the pan to the heat and bring to the boil, stirring until thickened. Remove the pan from the heat and beat in the egg yolks, 1 at a time. Add the cheese and stir until it has completely melted. Set the pan aside to cool.

3 Whisk the egg whites until just stiff enough to stand in peaks (see pages 22–23). Mix about 2 tablespoons of the egg whites into the cheese mixture, then carefully fold the remaining egg whites into the cheese mixture with a metal spoon (see page 23).

4 Grease a 1.5 litre/2½ pint soufflé dish with butter and place it on a baking sheet. Spread the cooled tomato mixture in the dish and cover with the soufflé mixture. Bake immediately in a preheated oven, 190°C/375°F/Gas Mark 5, for 35–40 minutes, until well risen and golden brown. Serve the soufflé immediately.

VARIATIONS • Instead of tomatoes, you could use 2 deseeded, peeled and thinly sliced or diced red peppers (see page 143).

Raspberry Meringue Nests

These individual pavlovas should be crisp on the outside and marshmallowy inside. The chocolate sauce, which may be served either warm or cold, can be spooned over just before serving.

Serves: **8**

Preparation time: 20 minutes

Cooking time: 50–55 minutes

Oven temperature: 140°C/275°F/Gas Mark 1

3 chocolate flakes
4 egg whites
200 g/7 oz caster sugar
1 teaspoon cornflour
1 teaspoon white wine vinegar
150 ml/¼ pint double cream
325 g/11 oz raspberries
SAUCE
200 g/7 oz plain chocolate, broken into pieces
4 tablespoons milk
3 tablespoons golden syrup
½ teaspoon vanilla essence
25 g/1 oz unsalted butter

1 Line a large baking sheet with non-stick baking paper. Coarsely crumble the chocolate flakes into a bowl.

2 Whisk the egg whites in a large bowl until stiff. Gradually whisk in the sugar, 1 tablespoon at a time, until the meringue is stiff and glossy. Stir in the cornflour, vinegar and two-thirds of the crumbled chocolate flakes. Divide the mixture into 8 mounds on the prepared baking sheet, spreading each one to about 7 cm/ 3 inches in diameter and making a dip in the centre. Bake in a preheated oven, 140°C/275°F/Gas Mark 1, for 45–50 minutes, until crisp. Set aside to cool.

3 For the sauce, put the chocolate, milk, golden syrup and vanilla essence into a small heavy-based saucepan and heat gently, stirring frequently, until the chocolate has melted. Stir in the butter. Continue stirring until the sauce is smooth, then pour it into a jug.

4 Whip the cream, fold in the raspberries and spoon the mixture on to the meringues. Decorate with the remaining crumbled chocolate flakes and serve with the sauce.

Sauces, Stocks and Soups

How to Make a Sauce

Roux-based Sauces

A roux is simply a mixture of flour and fat. Once cooked it will absorb and thicken a liquid giving a smooth consistency without lumps. It is the base for classic white sauces, such as béchamel. It is vital to cook the roux on its own before adding the liquid or the finished sauce will not be smooth.

Melt the butter in a saucepan, then stir in the flour and cook, stirring, for 1–2 minutes. The mixture should begin to bubble and form a honeycomb-like texture. Remove from the heat and gradually stir in the liquid, which may be either hot or cold. Return to the heat and continue stirring until the sauce boils. Simmer, stirring continuously, for a further 2–3 minutes, until the sauce is thickened and smooth.

All-in-One White Sauce

This is a quick and easy way to make a sauce with the same ingredients and proportions as the roux method, but the liquid must be cold.

Place the flour, butter and liquid in a saucepan and whisk with a balloon whisk over a moderate heat until boiling. Cook, stirring, for 2–3 minutes, until the sauce is thick and free of lumps.

Classic Béchamel Sauce
Makes: **300 ml/½ pint**
Preparation time: about 20 minutes
Cooking time: about 5 minutes

300 ml/½ pint milk
½ small onion, sliced
1 small carrot, sliced
small celery stick, sliced
6 peppercorns
1 bay leaf
15 g/½ oz butter

15 g/½ oz plain flour
salt and pepper
freshly grated nutmeg

1 Pour the milk into a saucepan and add the onion, carrot, celery, peppercorns and bay leaf. Heat the milk and flavouring ingredients over a low heat until almost boiling, then remove from the heat. Cover the pan and leave the milk to infuse for 10–15 minutes.
2 Strain the milk through a sieve and discard the flavouring ingredients. Make a roux from the butter and flour and cook, stirring, for 1–2 minutes. (Alternatively, leave the liquid until completely cold and make the sauce by the All-in-One method.)
3 Remove from the heat and gradually stir in the milk, then stir or whisk continuously over a moderate heat for 2–3 minutes, until the sauce boils and is smooth and thickened. Season to taste with salt, pepper and nutmeg.

VARIATIONS
Cheese Sauce
Stir 75 g/3 oz strong cheese, such as mature Cheddar, grated, and ½ teaspoon English or Dijon mustard into the finished sauce. Heat gently, stirring and without boiling, until the cheese melts.

Parsley Sauce
Stir 2 tablespoons finely chopped parsley into the finished sauce.

Mushroom Sauce
Finely slice 50 g/2 oz button mushrooms and cook them in 15 g/½ oz butter until soft. Stir into the finished sauce, adding a generous dash of Worcestershire sauce.

Basic Brown Sauces

Brown sauces are also made from a roux, the best-known classic brown sauce being gravy.

Cornflour-based Sauces

Sauces that are thickened with cornflour are made by the blending method. They have a fine, smooth texture which is particularly suitable for sweet sauces.

Basic Sweet White Sauce

Makes: **300 ml/½ pint**
Preparation time: 2 minutes
Cooking time: 2–3 minutes

4 teaspoons cornflour
2 tablespoons caster sugar
300 ml/½ pint milk
15 g/½ oz butter

1 Stir the cornflour and sugar together in a heatproof jug or a small bowl. Stir in just enough milk to make a smooth, thin paste.
2 Heat the remaining milk until almost boiling, then pour it into the paste stirring continuously.
3 Return the mixture to the saucepan and stir over a moderate heat until it boils. Then cook gently for 2–3 minutes, stirring until the sauce is thickened and smooth. Stir in the butter.

Vanilla Sauce

Place a vanilla pod in the saucepan when heating the milk. Set the milk aside to infuse for 15 minutes. Then reheat the milk and remove the vanilla pod before stirring it into the paste. Alternatively, add ½ teaspoon natural vanilla extract to the finished sauce.

Brandy or Rum Sauce

Add 2 tablespoons brandy or rum to the finished sauce.

Lemon or Orange Sauce

Stir the finely grated rind of 1 lemon or orange into the finished sauce.

How to Make Perfect Gravy

The best gravy is made in the roasting tin after meat or poultry has been roasted and using the tasty juices for flavour. The amount of flour can be adjusted depending on how thick you like your gravy.

1 Carefully pour as much fat as possible from the roasting tin, leaving behind the cooking juices and sediment.
2 Sprinkle 1–2 tablespoons plain flour into the tin and stir to mix it into the juices. Place the tin over the heat and stir the roux continuously for 1–2 minutes, until it is bubbling.
3 Gradually stir in about 300 ml/½ pint stock or vegetable cooking water, then stir until the gravy boils. Cook for 2–3 minutes, still stirring, until the gravy is thickened and smooth. Taste and adjust the seasoning before serving.

Enriching Gravy

For a richly flavoured gravy, deglaze the roasting tin by stirring in 2–3 tablespoons red or white wine, port or sherry after step 1.

Heat, stirring and scraping up the residue, then allow to boil for a few minutes to reduce the liquid and concentrate the flavour. Sprinkle in the flour and continue as above.

Redcurrant or cranberry jelly is also delicious in gravy, particularly to serve with roast lamb or poultry. Add 1 tablespoon jelly when the gravy has boiled and stir until melted.

Baked Lasagne with Meat

Baking is the most usual way of cooking lasagne, and sheets of lasagne layered with minced beef and béchamel sauces is the most widely known way of baking it (indeed, the dish is frequently referred to simply as lasagne).

Serves: **4–6**

Preparation time: 20 minutes

Cooking time: 2–2¼ hours

Oven temperature: 180°C/350°F/Gas Mark 4

2 x quantity Classic Béchamel Sauce (see page 30)

250 g/8 oz lasagne verde or no pre-cook lasagne

75 g/3 oz Parmesan cheese, freshly grated

salt and pepper

MINCED BEEF SAUCE

4½ teaspoons olive oil

40 g/1½ oz pancetta or streaky bacon, finely chopped

1 small onion, finely chopped

1 large garlic clove, finely chopped

½ small carrot, finely chopped

1 small celery stick, finely chopped

125 ml/4 fl oz medium-bodied dry white wine

275 g/9 oz lean minced beef

4 tablespoons milk

300 g/10 oz beefsteak tomatoes, chopped

1 tablespoon torn basil leaves

FOOD FACT • Pancetta is a fatty bacon, widely used in many Italian dishes. It may be smoked or unsmoked, in a single piece or sliced. It adds a special depth of flavour and is an essential ingredient for authenticity. However, streaky bacon is quite a good substitute.

1 First make the minced beef sauce. Heat the oil in a small, heavy flameproof casserole. Add the pancetta or bacon, onion, garlic, carrot and celery and fry, stirring occasionally, until the onion and garlic are soft and translucent. Stir in the wine and allow to bubble gently until almost evaporated.

2 Stir in the meat, breaking it up with a fork. Cook gently until it has all changed colour, then stir in the milk and continue to cook over a low heat, stirring frequently, until the milk has evaporated. Stir in the tomatoes and season to taste with salt and pepper. Heat almost to simmering point, cover and cook over a very low heat, stirring frequently, for about 1 hour. Uncover and continue to cook until there is no free liquid and the sauce is concentrated. Stir in the basil.

3 If not using no pre-cook lasagne, bring a large saucepan of lightly salted water to the boil, add the lasagne, stir, cover and return to the boil. If using fresh lasagne, boil for 3 minutes, if using dried, 7–8 minutes. Do not overcook or it will be soggy. Drain well and rinse under cold running water. If using no pre-cook lasagne, follow the packet instructions.

4 Spread about one quarter of the minced beef sauce evenly over the base of a large, shallow, ovenproof dish, about 18 x 24 cm/ 7 x 9½ inches. Cover with approximately one-quarter of the béchamel sauce, then arrange a single layer of lasagne on top. Repeat with the remaining ingredients, finishing with a layer of béchamel sauce. Cover this with Parmesan cheese and bake in a preheated oven, 180°C/350°F/Gas Mark 4, for about 30–35 minutes. Serve immediately, straight from the dish.

Seafood Pie

Every cook has a recipe for fish and potato pie because, whatever the version, it is delicious, nourishing and easy to make. This impressive-looking recipe combines smoked fish, white fish fillets and prawns topped with overlapping potato slices rather than the more usual layer of mashed potato.

Serves: **6–8**

Preparation time: 15 minutes

Cooking time: about 1 hour

Oven temperature: 200°C/400°F/Gas Mark 6

750 g/1½ lb waxy potatoes
40 g/1½ oz butter, plus extra for dotting
50 g/2 oz plain flour
1 teaspoon mustard powder
450 ml/¾ pint milk
75 g/3 oz Gruyère cheese, grated
2 tablespoons olive oil
1 onion, finely chopped
grated rind of 1 lime
2 celery sticks, finely sliced
125 g/4 oz button mushrooms, halved
375 g/12 oz smoked haddock or cod fillet, skinned (see page 91) and cubed
375 g/12 oz cod fillet, skinned (see page 91) and cubed
250 g/8 oz cooked peeled prawns
2 tablespoons chopped dill
2 tablespoons chopped parsley
salt and pepper

1 Cook the potatoes in a large saucepan of lightly salted boiling water for 8–10 minutes until parboiled. Drain, refresh under cold water and slice thinly. Set aside. Grease a deep 1.8 litre/3 pint ovenproof dish.

2 Melt the butter in a saucepan. Stir in the flour and mustard powder and cook, stirring constantly, for 30 seconds. Gradually beat in the milk until smooth. Continue to stir over a low heat until the sauce boils. Simmer for 2 minutes, remove from the heat and stir in 50 g/2 oz of the cheese. Cover the surface of the sauce with baking paper.

3 Heat the oil in a saucepan. Add the onion, lime rind and celery and fry, stirring occasionally, for 5 minutes, until softened. Add the mushrooms and fry, stirring frequently, for 2–3 minutes, until browned. Remove the pan from the heat and set aside to cool.

4 Stir the sauce, fish, prawns, dill and parsley into the onion and mushroom mixture and season to taste with salt and pepper. Pour the filling into the prepared dish.

5 Arrange the potatoes in overlapping slices over the filling. Dot with butter and sprinkle over the remaining cheese.

6 Cover the pie with foil and bake in a preheated oven, 200°C/400°F/Gas Mark 6, for 30 minutes. Remove the foil and continue to bake for a further 20–25 minutes, until the cheese is bubbling and golden.

How to Make Egg-based and Uncooked Sauces

Classic Mayonnaise

Makes: **approx 300 ml/½ pint**
Preparation time: about 10 minutes

2 egg yolks
1 teaspoon Dijon mustard
2 teaspoons white wine vinegar
pinch of caster sugar
salt and pepper
300 ml/½ pint olive oil

1 Place the egg yolks, mustard, vinegar, sugar, salt and pepper in a mixing bowl and whisk lightly until combined.
2 Gradually add the oil, drop by drop at first, whisking continuously until the mixture begins to thicken.
3 When the mixture has thickened slightly, add the remaining oil in a thin, steady stream, still whisking until all the oil is incorporated and the mayonnaise is thick. Adjust the seasoning to taste.

TIP • If the mayonnaise starts to curdle, beat a fresh egg yolk in a clean bowl, then gradually whisk in the curdled mayonnaise, a spoonful at a time, until the mixture thickens.

Blender Mayonnaise
Place the egg yolks, mustard, vinegar, sugar, salt and pepper in a blender and process for a few seconds to mix thoroughly. With the motor running, gradually add the oil in a thin stream through the feeder tube in the lid. Process until the mayonnaise is smooth and thick.

VARIATIONS
Aïoli
Omit the mustard from the basic recipe and add 4 garlic cloves, crushed, to the yolks.

Herb Mayonnaise
Stir 3 tablespoons mixed finely chopped fresh basil, parsley and chives into the prepared mayonnaise. Alternatively, you can add the herbs to the blender for the final few seconds of processing.

Blue Cheese Dressing
Stir 50 g/2 oz Stilton or Gorgonzola cheese, crumbled with your fingers or mashed, into the prepared mayonnaise.

Lemon Mayonnaise
Replace the wine vinegar with lemon juice. Stir in 1 teaspoon finely grated lemon rind and 1 tablespoon freshly squeezed lemon juice to the prepared mayonnaise.

Reduced-fat Mayonnaise
Use 1 whole egg instead of 3 yolks. Alternatively, you can mix the prepared mayonnaise with an equal quantity of low-fat natural yogurt.

Speedy Blender Hollandaise Sauce

Makes: about 200 ml/7 fl oz
Preparation time: about 5 minutes, plus cooling

150 g/5 oz butter
1 tablespoon white wine vinegar or lemon juice
3 egg yolks
salt and pepper
lemon juice to taste

1 Melt the butter then remove it from the heat and allow to cool, but not set.

2 Place the wine vinegar or lemon juice, egg yolks, salt and pepper in a blender and process for about 10 seconds on high speed.
3 With the motor running at high speed, add the butter in a thin, steady stream through the lid of the blender.
4 Add lemon juice to taste and serve at once.

TIP • If the Hollandaise Sauce begins to curdle and separate, place a spoonful of vinegar in a clean bowl and gradually whisk in the sauce until it thickens.

Simple Uncooked Sauces

How to Make a Salsa

Salsas can be made from almost any fresh vegetables or fruit, coarsely or finely chopped, or processed almost to a purée in a food processor. The simplest is Salsa Cruda, 'raw sauce', but you can try your own choice of ingredients. Serve with salads, grilled fish, meat or poultry or with fresh bread and cheese.

Basic Salsa Cruda

Makes about: **400 ml/14 fl oz**
Preparation time: 5 minutes

1 garlic clove
1 small red onion
2 fresh green chillies
375 g/12 oz tomatoes
2 tablespoons chopped fresh coriander
salt and pepper
lime or lemon juice to taste

Chop all the ingredients with a knife or in a food processor. Mix them together, adding seasoning and lime or lemon juice, to taste.

Salsa Combinations

Mango, roasted red pepper and root ginger
Green pepper, spring onion and celery
Orange, banana and chilli
Avocado, chilli, lime and coriander

How to Make Perfect Pesto

The best pesto is made by hand, using a pestle and mortar and with the freshest ingredients. If time is short, you can put all the ingredients in a food processor and pulse the power on and off for a few seconds. Do not over-process the mixture or the pesto will be too smooth.

Classic pesto is made from pine nuts, basil and Parmesan cheese, but walnuts or hazelnuts, coriander and Pecorino cheese can be used instead to make an alternative, slightly more economical version. Other herbs can replace the basil, for example rocket or coriander.

Classic Pesto alla Genovese

Serves: **4**
Preparation time: 10 minutes

25 g/1 oz pine nuts
50 g/2 oz fresh basil leaves
2 garlic cloves, chopped
pinch of sea salt
50 g/2 oz freshly grated Parmesan cheese
100 ml/3½ fl oz extra virgin olive oil

1 Lightly toast the pine nuts until pale golden, then leave to cool.
2 Place the basil, garlic, pine nuts and salt in a mortar and pound the mixture to a coarse pulp using a pestle.
3 Gradually add the cheese, pounding it into the pulp to make a thick paste.
4 Add the oil a little at a time, pounding it with the pestle into the mixture until it is all thoroughly incorporated.

How to Make Perfect Stock

However easy stock cubes may be, there is nothing to beat the flavour of real home-made stock. It is cheap and simple to make and it freezes well, ready to add flavour to all your sauces, soups and stews.

Rules for Good Stock

1 For a clear stock, it is important to skim off the scum which gathers on the surface during cooking, as the fat and impurities from which it is formed will make the liquid cloudy.

2 Avoid adding potatoes, as these tend to break down and make the stock cloudy.

3 Boiling concentrates the flavours, so keep seasoning light. It is easier and better to adjust the seasoning of the finished dish.

4 Strain the cooked stock through a fine sieve. If you do not have a suitable sieve, line an ordinary sieve with muslin and let the stock drain through it. Do not press the vegetables through or they will make the stock cloudy.

Basic Beef Stock

Makes: **1.5 litres/2¾ pints**
Preparation time: 15 minutes
Cooking time: 4½ hours

750 g/1½ lb shin of beef, diced
2 onions, chopped
2 carrots, chopped
2 celery sticks, chopped
1 bouquet garni
6 black peppercorns
1.8 litres/3 pints cold water

Place all the ingredients in a large saucepan and bring slowly to the boil. Reduce the heat until the stock simmers slowly. Skim any scum from the surface, then cover the pan and simmer for 4 hours. Strain and cool the cooked stock.

Basic Chicken Stock

Makes: 1 litre/1¾ pints
Preparation time: 10 minutes
Cooking time: about 2½ hours

1 cooked chicken carcass
chicken giblets (optional)
1 onion, chopped
2 carrots, chopped
1 celery stick, chopped
1 bouquet garni
1 teaspoon black peppercorns
½ teaspoon salt
1.8 litres/3 pints cold water

Cut the chicken carcass into 3–4 pieces and place them in a large saucepan with the remaining ingredients. Bring to the boil and skim off any scum. Reduce the heat, cover and simmer gently for 2–2½ hours. Strain and cool the stock.

Basic Fish Stock

Makes: 1 litre/1¾ pints
Preparation time: 10 minutes
Cooking time: 20 minutes

1 kg/2 lb white fish bones and trimmings
1 onion, sliced
2 carrots, sliced
2 celery sticks, sliced
1 bouquet garni
6 white peppercorns
½ teaspoon salt
150 ml/¼ pint dry white wine
1 litre/1¾ pints cold water

Place all the ingredients in a large saucepan and bring slowly to the boil. Skim off any scum, then reduce the heat and cover the pan. Simmer very gently for 20 minutes. Strain and cool the stock.

Basic Vegetable Stock

Makes: 1 litre/1¾ pints
Preparation time: 10 minutes
Cooking time: 45 minutes

500 g/1 lb mixed vegetables, chopped, for
  example onions, carrots, celery and leeks
1 litre/1¾ pints water
1 garlic clove
6 black peppercorns
1 bouquet garni
½ teaspoon salt

Place all the ingredients in a large saucepan and bring slowly to the boil. Skim off any scum, then reduce the heat and cover the pan. Simmer gently for 30 minutes. Strain and cool the stock.

Removing Fat from Stock

A small amount of fat usually collects on the surface of most stocks as they cook and this should be removed before use. If the stock is still warm, use a large spoon to skim off as much fat as possible, then add a few ice cubes. The fat will set around the ice and it is then easy to spoon it out. Alternatively, cool and chill the stock until the fat sets in a layer on the surface, then it is easy to lift off.

Storing Stock

To store stock, reduce it first by boiling it rapidly, uncovered, until reduced by about half. This concentrates the flavour and saves storage space. For food safety, cool stocks as quickly as possible, then cover and chill them. Stock will keep in the refrigerator for 2–3 days or it may be frozen for longer storage.

To freeze stock in convenient portions for use in sauces, casseroles and similar dishes, pour it into ice cube trays and freeze until solid, then tip the cubes of concentrated stock into polythene bags to store.

How to Make Soups

It is a popular myth that soups require hours of preparation; in fact, most take only a few minutes' attention, especially if you have a food processor or blender to purée velvet-smooth cream soups. Making soup is so rewarding, with plenty of scope for sampling creative flavour combinations. Soups are also versatile – they can be quick and simple mid-day snacks; hearty, nutritious family main courses; or elegant dinner party starters.

The secret of most good soups is a well-flavoured stock, so start by either making your own stock or buying a good-quality product. Then choose the freshest vegetables in season for the best flavour and most economical result.

Basic Creamed Carrot Soup

Serves: **6**
Preparation time: about 15 minutes
Cooking time: 25–35 minutes

40 g/1½ oz butter
1 large onion, chopped
750 g /1½ lb carrots, chopped
2 celery sticks, chopped
30 ml/2 tablespoons sherry or dry white wine (optional)
1.2 litres/2 pints stock, plus extra for thinning
salt and pepper

1 Melt the butter in a heavy-based pan, add the onion and fry over a moderate heat, stirring often, until just turning golden brown.
2 Add the carrots and celery with the sherry or white wine (if using). Reduce the heat to low, cover the pan tightly and allow the vegetables to 'sweat' for 15–20 minutes, shaking the pan occasionally to prevent them from sticking.
3 Stir in the stock, then bring to the boil. If necessary, reduce the heat and simmer for

10–15 minutes, until the vegetables are tender.
4 Purée the mixture in a food processor or blender until smooth. Alternatively, press the

mixture through a sieve, using the back of a ladle or wooden spoon to rub the vegetables through the mesh.
5 Return the soup to the rinsed-out pan. Taste and adjust the seasoning, then heat until boiling, adding a little more stock or cream to thin the soup to the desired consistency.

Thickening with *Beurre Manié*

The easiest way to thicken a soup after cooking is to use *beurre manié*. This is a paste of plain flour and butter, which is whisked into simmering liquid in small pieces. As the butter melts, the flour is incorporated smoothly and the liquid is thickened without lumps. *Beurre manié* is also useful for thickening cooking juices, sauces, stews and casseroles. It is worth making a large batch since it keeps well in the refrigerator.

Cream equal amounts of butter and plain flour together to form a thick, smooth paste. Drop small pieces or teaspoonfuls of the paste into the barely simmering soup, stirring briskly and continously until each piece of paste has melted and is completely incorporated before adding the next. Simmer for 2–3 minutes, stirring, until the soup is thickened.

Freezing Soups

Most soups freeze successfully and they keep well for 2–3 months. Highly seasoned or garlic-flavoured soups are best used within 2–3 weeks, since the flavour may be affected.

Pack soups for the freezer in rigid containers with well-fitting lids, in 300–600 ml/½–1 pint quantities which will thaw quickly and easily. Remember to allow room for the soup to expand in the container – at least 3 cm/1¼ inches of headspace. Seal and label clearly with type of soup and date.

Cheese

A sprinkling of grated Cheddar, Gruyère or Parmesan cheese adds flavour to vegetable soups. Try crumbling feta cheese or finely dicing mozzarella cheese for topping soups with Mediterranean flavours.

Pesto or Tapenade

A swirl of Pesto alla Genovese (see page 37) or tapenade (olive paste), either homemade or bought, adds an intense flavour to simple vegetable soups.

Flavoured Oils

At the last minute, drizzle a little flavoured oil, such as chilli oil, basil oil or lemon oil, on to the soup. This is particularly delicious with cold soups, for example Gazpacho (a purée of fresh tomatoes, peppers, cucumber and onion thickened with breadcrumbs).

Garnishes and Additions for Soups

Most soups benefit from finishing touches that add a contrast in colour, texture and/or flavour to transform even the plainest bowl of soup into your own special creation. These ideas are suitable for most soups.

Cream or Crème Fraîche

Swirl a spoonful into each portion of soup; for an extra flourish, particularly in smooth soups, use a cocktail stick to swirl the cream into a delicate feather pattern.

Herbs

Scatter a handful of chopped parsley, snipped chives or torn basil leaves over soup just before serving it.

Citrus Rind

Use a zester to pare fine curls of lemon, lime or orange rind off the fruit and scatter it over soup for colour and flavour. For example, orange rind goes well with carrot soup or lime rind is delicious on avocado soup.

Croûtons

Remove the crusts from sliced white or wholemeal bread and use a sharp knife to cut the slices into 1 cm/½ inch squares. Alternatively, use small food cutters to stamp out bread shapes, such as hearts, stars or flower shapes. Quickly stir-fry the pieces of bread in a mixture of butter and oil until crisp and golden brown. Drain on kitchen paper and sprinkle over the soup just before serving.

Cream of Sweetcorn Soup

This tasty soup can be made very quickly from storecupboard ingredients. Crumbled fried bacon or croûtons make an attractive garnish, contrasting in texture with the creaminess of the soup.

Serves: **4–6**

Preparation time: 5–10 minutes

Cooking time: about 30 minutes

40 g/1½ oz butter
1 onion, chopped
2 potatoes, diced
25 g/1 oz plain flour
900 ml/1½ pints milk
1 bay leaf
2 x 326 g/11½ oz cans sweetcorn, drained
2 tablespoons double cream
salt and pepper
crumbled fried bacon, to garnish

1 Melt the butter in a large saucepan. Add the onion and cook over a low heat, stirring frequently, for 5 minutes, without browning. Add the potatoes and cook for a further 2 minutes.

2 Stir in the flour, then gradually add the milk, stirring constantly. Bring to the boil, add the bay leaf and season with salt and pepper to taste. Add half of the sweetcorn, cover and simmer for 15–20 minutes.

3 Remove and discard the bay leaf and set aside to cool slightly. Rub the soup through a strainer or process in a blender until smooth. Return to the pan, add the remaining sweetcorn and heat through.

4 Stir in the cream, sprinkle over the bacon and serve immediately.

FOOD FACT • To make garlic croûtons, cut the crusts off 2 slices white bread and gently rub the bread all over with the cut sides of a halved garlic clove, then cube the bread. Heat ½ tablespoon vegetable oil and a knob of butter in a heavy-based frying pan and fry the bread cubes, turning and stirring frequently, for 1–2 minutes, until golden and crisp.

Minestrone Soup

This classic soup exists in as many forms as there are cooks in Italy. A mixture of vegetables and beans forms the basis and spaghetti, small pasta shapes or rice are added to the soup towards the end of the cooking time.

Serves: **4**

Preparation time: 5 minutes

Cooking time: 25 minutes

2 tablespoons olive oil
1 onion, diced
1 garlic clove, crushed
2 celery sticks, chopped
1 leek, finely sliced
1 carrot, chopped
400 g/13 oz can chopped tomatoes
600 ml/1 pint Chicken or Vegetable Stock
  (see page 39)
1 courgette, diced
½ small cabbage, shredded
1 bay leaf
75 g/3 oz canned haricot beans
75 g/3 oz dried spaghetti, broken in to small
  pieces or small pasta shapes
1 tablespoon chopped flat leaf parsley
salt and pepper
50 g/2 oz Parmesan cheese, freshly grated,
  to serve

1 Heat the oil in a large saucepan. Add the onion, garlic, celery, leek and carrot and sauté over a medium heat, stirring occasionally, for 3 minutes.

2 Add the tomatoes, stock, courgette, cabbage, bay leaf and haricot beans. Bring to the boil, lower the heat and simmer for 10 minutes.

3 Add the pasta and season to taste with salt and pepper. Stir well and cook for a further 8 minutes. Keep stirring since the soup may stick to the base of the pan.

4 Just before serving, add the chopped parsley and stir well. Ladle into warm soup bowls and serve with grated Parmesan.

Hot and Sour Soup

This popular Oriental-style soup is wonderfully warming. Traditionally, it can be quite complicated with lots of different ingredients, but this is a quick-and-easy version, made hot with fresh red chilli rather than the more usual pepper.

Serves: **6–8**

Preparation time: 10 minutes, plus soaking

Cooking time: about 15 minutes

about 15 g/½ oz dried shiitake or other wild mushrooms
125 ml/4 fl oz hot water
125–175 g/4–6 oz boneless cooked chicken
1 litre/1¾ pints Chicken Stock (see page 39)
2–3 tablespoons rice wine vinegar or white wine or cider vinegar
2–3 tablespoons light soy sauce
1 teaspoon sugar
1 red chilli, deseeded and very finely sliced or chopped
4 spring onions, very finely sliced diagonally
2 teaspoons cornflour
2 tablespoons cold water

1 Soak the dried mushrooms in the hot water for 35–40 minutes. Drain the mushrooms and reserve the soaking water. Finely slice the mushrooms, discarding any hard stalks. Shred the cooked chicken with your fingers

2 Bring the stock to the boil in a large saucepan. Add 2 tablespoons each of vinegar and soy sauce, then add the sugar, mushrooms and the reserved mushroom soaking water. Simmer for 5 minutes. Add half the chilli and half the spring onions, stir well and simmer for 5 minutes.

3 Add the shredded chicken, stir and heat through for 1–2 minutes. Mix together the cornflour and water to a smooth paste, then pour it into the soup and stir to mix. Simmer, stirring constantly, for 1–2 minutes until the soup thickens.

4 Taste and add more vinegar and more soy sauce, if liked. Serve piping hot, sprinkled with the remaining chilli and spring onions.

FOOD FACT • Shiitake mushrooms have a distinctive flavour and aroma. When sold dried, they are sometimes also known simply as Chinese mushrooms. Alternatively, you can use fresh shiitake or other wild mushrooms, or button mushrooms, and omit the soaking.

Pasta and Noodles

Types of Pasta and Noodles

Long Round Pasta

These include the familiar spaghetti, buccatini and macaroni, which are made by extruding long strands of the dough. These pastas are traditionally served with meat sauces, *ragu* and tomato-based mixtures. Ziti or zitoni is the broadest of these and is useful served with rich meaty sauces. The finest, traditionally gathered and dried into nests, is cappellini (fine hair) or *cappelli di angelo*, angel's hair pasta, which should be used with light sauces or in broths.

Flat Pasta

Pasta dough is rolled and cut to various widths to make ribbon pasta. The narrowest linguini, followed by slightly broader fettucine and tagliatelle, then broad-cut papardelle and sheets of lasagne or wide ribbons of lasagnette. The thicker ribbon pastas are ideal for egg-based sauces, such as carbonara, as the larger smooth surface area of hot freshly cooked pasta helps to set the lightly cooked egg quickly. Wide noodles are also good with tomato, cream or Bolognese-type sauces; the finer ones, such as linguine, are best with pesto or light tomato sauce.

Pasta comes in hundreds of types, shapes, sizes and colours, both fresh and dried. Dried pasta is extremely convenient and is in no way inferior to fresh pasta – in fact, many good-quality types of dried pasta are far superior to some of the commercial fresh pasta available.

Basic Dried Pasta

Dried pasta can be used for the majority of recipes, with the exception of filled pasta such as ravioli. Look for pasta made with 100% durum wheat, *pasta di semolina grano duro* in Italian, since it has a good, firm texture. Some types include eggs, *pasta all'uova*, but eggs are more commonly used in fresh pasta doughs.

Italian-style Pasta

The different shapes fall broadly into four categories.

Short Pasta

This group includes many of the most familiar shapes, such as penne (pens or quills), farfalle (bows or butterflies), conchiglie (shells), fusilli (spirals) and cut or 'elbow' macaroni. These are best served with tomato or meat sauces, as their shapes trap the sauce well.

Very Short Pasta or 'Pastina'

These are very small pasta shapes used in soups and broths, including lumachine (little snails), stelline (stars) and ditalini (thimbles).

boiled for 3–6 minutes, depending on thickness, but the boiled noodles can also be either shallow or deep-fried.

Rice noodles

There is a wide variety, including rice sticks. These are fine, brittle noodles made from rice flour. They may be soaked and drained, then added to soups and other dishes, or deep-fried straight from the packet.

Cellophane Noodles

These are made from mung beans, which are cooked and puréed and dried into sheets, then pressed into noodles. Soak for a few minutes before adding to stir-fries or soups, or dry thoroughly and deep-fry until crisp.

Japanese Noodles

As well as egg noodles, which are the same as the Chinese egg noodles, there are several types of Japanese noodles. Soba noodles are thin noodles traditionally made from buckwheat flour. Udon are thicker, white noodles made from wheat flour. Somen are thinner wheat noodles. Japanese noodles are usually boiled or soaked and served with dipping sauces or in light broth.

Filled Pasta

Filled pasta comes in a wide variety of shapes and sizes, with an infinite choice of fish, meat, vegetable or cheese fillings. Ravioli is, perhaps, the most familiar; smaller ravioli are known as ravioletti or raviolini. Agnolotti are small circles, filled and folded in half to make crescent shapes, cappaletti look like pinched three-cornered hats and tortellini are round shapes with the larger version known as tortelloni.

Speciality Pastas

There is also a huge array of imaginatively shaped, coloured and flavoured pastas available. Green pasta, *verde*, is made by adding spinach purée; red, *rossa*, has tomato purée or beetroot added; and *pasta nera*, the black pasta, has squid ink added to the dough. Three-colour pasta, *tricolore*, consists of green, red and plain pasta shapes.

There are also many types of pasta flavoured with mushrooms, truffles, herbs and spices, to add interest and variety to your dishes. You can even buy chocolate pasta with added cocoa, which makes an unusual and surprisingly tasty dessert!

As well as the flavoured doughs, there are many traditional international types of pasta made from ingredients other than wheat. Buckwheat pasta, corn- and rice-based pasta are all readily available.

Oriental Noodles

Chinese Egg Noodles

These are made with wheat flour and eggs, and are widely used in Chinese and Thai cookery. They are usually dried and packed in rectangular sheets, but Oriental shops often sell them fresh. They can be simply served

How to Make Pasta

If you have never tried making your own pasta, then do have a go as it is a very simple and rewarding process. You do not need a special pasta-making machine since the dough can be rolled and cut by hand. If you plan to make pasta very often, a pasta machine may prove to be a useful investment.

Basic Pasta Dough

Serves:
Preparation time: about 15 minutes, plus resting

300 g/10 oz pasta flour or strong plain flour
pinch of salt
3 eggs

1 Sift the flour and salt into a mound on a work surface and make a well in the centre.
2 Break the eggs into the well and use your fingertips or a fork to work the ingredients together, gradually working the flour in from the sides into the eggs and mixing to form a soft paste. If the pasta is too sticky, work in a little extra flour. Draw the dough together to form a ball.

3 Wash your hands thoroughly, then wash and dry the work surface. Dust the work surface lightly with flour. Knead the dough for about 10 minutes or until it is completely smooth and elastic.
4 Wrap the dough in clingfilm and leave it to rest for 20–30 minutes before use, but do not place it in the refrigerator.

VARIATIONS
Tomato Pasta
Add 2 tablespoons concentrated tomato purée with the eggs.

Spinach Pasta

Thaw 150 g/5 oz frozen chopped spinach and press out as much moisture as possible in a fine sieve. Add the spinach with the eggs.

Saffron Pasta

Infuse a pinch of saffron strands in 1 tablespoon boiling water. Cool and add to the basic dough with the eggs.

Garlic and Herb Pasta

Add 1 garlic clove, finely crushed, and 1 tablespoon finely chopped fresh herbs with the eggs.

Rolling, Cutting and Filling Pasta

The pasta dough should be used or cooked immediately for stuffed pasta, such as ravioli, or for lasagne sheets, but cut shapes should be allowed to dry for 5–10 minutes before cooking. Do not allow the pasta to dry for too long, or it will become brittle and break easily.

If you make pasta often, it is worth investing in a small hand-operated pasta machine which has attachments for rolling dough and cutting different basic shapes. Roll out the dough on a lightly floured surface to 2–3 mm/$\frac{1}{16}$–$\frac{1}{8}$ inch thick, then cut it into noodles or lasagne.

Tagliatelle or Noodles

Cut the rolled pasta sheets into 25–30 cm/ 10–12 inch lengths, then roll up the pieces fairly loosely, like a Swiss roll, and slice them with a sharp knife. The thickness of the slices determines the width of the noodles. Shake out the cut slices to separate the noodles.

Lasagne or Cannelloni

Cut the rolled pasta sheets into 10 x 15 cm/ 4 x 6 inch rectangles. When making cannelloni, the cooked pieces of pasta are rolled around the filling.

Making Ravioli

1 Roll out the dough to 2 thin sheets of the same size. Cover 1 sheet with clingfilm while putting filling on the other sheet.

2 Working quickly to prevent the pasta drying out, place teaspoonfuls of filling in rows over the pasta. Keep the mounds of filling and rows evenly spaced at 3.5 cm/1½ inch intervals.

3 Brush a little egg white or water between the piles of filling.

4 Carefully lay the second sheet of dough over the top, avoiding stretching it. Use your fingers to press firmly between the mounds of stuffing to seal them between the sheets of stuffing.

5 Using a knife or pasta cutting wheel, cut between the stuffing to make ravioli squares. Leave to dry for 20–30 minutes before use.

Cooking Pasta

There are just a few simple rules for cooking perfect pasta and they apply to both fresh and dried types.

1 Use a large saucepan, allowing 2 litres/ 3½ pints water to each 200 g/7 oz pasta. If you do not have a large enough pan, use the largest you have and make sure there is plenty of water to allow the pasta to move while it cooks.

2 Bring the water to a fast, rolling boil before adding the pasta.

3 Add the salt at the same time as you add

the pasta – about 2 teaspoons to each 2 litres/3½ pints water. Add the pasta quickly, stirring once to prevent it sticking together, then bring back to the boil quickly.

4 To cook long pasta, such as spaghetti, hold the pasta in a bunch and hold it in the boiling water, gradually lowering it as it softens.

5 Cooking times vary according to the type and shape of pasta. Fresh pasta takes 2–3 minutes; dried pasta 8–12 minutes. The best way to check if pasta is cooked is to taste a piece – it should be tender, but still slightly firm to the bite, or *al dente* as the Italians say.

6 Drain the pasta immediately it is cooked, turning it into a colander. When cooking filled pasta, such as ravioli, use a slotted spoon to remove the pieces as they are cooked.

7 Toss the pasta in a little butter or oil to prevent the pieces from sticking together or toss with a sauce and serve.

Making Gnocchi

Gnocchi are classed as pasta even though they are in fact miniature dumplings. They can be made from potatoes, semolina or soft cheese. Potato gnocchi are very simple to make: the secret of success is to keep all the ingredients very cold. For the best texture, choose a floury variety of potatoes, such as Maris Piper.

Potato Gnocchi

Serves: **6**
Preparation time: 15 minutes plus resting
Cooking time: 3–4 minutes

1 kg/2 lb potatoes
salt and pepper
1 egg, beaten
1 tablespoon olive oil
250 g/8 oz plain flour

1 Cook the potatoes in their skins in lightly salted boiling water for about 20 minutes or until tender. Drain and leave to cool.

2 Remove the skins and mash the potatoes thoroughly or press them through a sieve into a bowl. Make a well in the centre and add the seasoning, egg, oil and half the flour. Mix the ingredients until the flour is incorporated, then gradually knead in the remaining flour until you have a soft, smooth dough. Cover and leave the dough to rest for about 15 minutes.

3 Cut the dough in half and roll 2 long sausages, about 2.5 cm/1 inch in diameter. Cut the rolls into 1.5 cm/¾ inch lengths. Press each piece into a neat oval over the prongs of a fork.

4 Heat a large saucepan of salted water and cook the gnocchi in batches for 3–4 minutes, until they float to the surface. Drain and serve with butter and grated Parmesan cheese, or with a pasta sauce.

Spaghetti Carbonara

Quick, easy, inexpensive and utterly delicious – what more could anyone ask for? The secret of success with this dish is to make sure that all the ingredients are kept piping hot, so that the eggs cook as soon as they touch the pan.

Serves: **4**

Preparation time: 10 minutes

Cooking time: 15 minutes

1 tablespoon olive oil
175 g/6 oz smoked bacon, rinds removed and cut into strips
1 garlic clove, crushed
300 g/10 oz spaghetti
4 tablespoons double cream
3 egg yolks
75 g/3 oz Parmesan cheese, freshly grated
salt and pepper

1 Heat the oil in a heavy-based saucepan. Add the bacon and cook over a low heat, stirring occasionally, for 3 minutes. Add the garlic and cook for 1 minute.
2 Bring a large saucepan of lightly salted water to the boil. Add the spaghetti and cook for 3–4 minutes if fresh, or 8 minutes if dried, until tender, but still firm to the bite. Drain and return to the pan.
3 Beat the cream and egg yolks together, add to the bacon and mix well over a very low heat, but do not allow the eggs to scramble.
4 Add the sauce and Parmesan to the spaghetti, season to taste with salt and pepper and toss well with two forks. Mix thoroughly and serve immediately.

VARIATION • For extra flavour, add 125 g/ 4 oz sliced mushrooms to the pan with the bacon and fry over a low heat, stirring occasionally, for 5 minutes.

Ricotta and Spinach Cannelloni

Ricotta is an Italian whey cheese with a creamy texture and bland, slightly sweet flavour. It is widely used in sweet and savoury Italian dishes and forms a classic partnership with spinach.

Serves: 3–4

Preparation time: 15 minutes

Cooking time: 1 hour–1 hour 10 minutes

Oven temperature: 180°C/350°F/Gas Mark 4

butter, for greasing
250 g/8 oz fresh spinach
125 g/4 oz ricotta cheese
3 tablespoons grated Parmesan cheese
pinch of grated nutmeg
1 egg yolk
1 tablespoon chopped mixed herbs, such as marjoram, chives, parsley and chervil
6–8 cannelloni tubes
salt and pepper
TOMATO SAUCE
500 g/1 lb ripe tomatoes, skinned and chopped
1 small onion, chopped
1 celery stick, chopped
1 tablespoon tomato purée
½ teaspoon sugar
salt and pepper

1 Grease a shallow ovenproof dish with the butter. Put the spinach in a saucepan with just the water that clings to the leaves after washing. Cover and cook for 7–10 minutes, shaking the pan occasionally, until the spinach is tender. Drain well, squeezing out as much liquid as possible, and chop finely.

2 Place the spinach in a bowl with the ricotta, 1 tablespoon of the Parmesan, the nutmeg, egg yolk and herbs and season with salt and pepper to taste. Mix thoroughly.

3 Carefully fill the cannelloni tubes with the spinach mixture, using a small teaspoon. Place in the prepared dish in a single layer.

4 Put all the tomato sauce ingredients in a heavy-based saucepan. Bring to the boil, reduce the heat and cook for 20 minutes. If liked, press through a sieve or process in a blender or food processor until fairly smooth.

5 Pour the tomato sauce evenly over the cannelloni, ensuring they are all covered. Sprinkle with the remaining Parmesan cheese.

6 Bake in a preheated oven, 180°C/350°F/Gas Mark 4, for 35–40 minutes, until the cannelloni are tender (test by piercing with a sharp pointed knife). Serve immediately.

Chow Mein

A wok is perfect for stir-frying because its rounded shape ensures that food cooks evenly and rapidly, but you can use a frying pan. Make sure the wok or pan is very hot before adding any ingredients and keep stirring and tossing them from the middle to the sides.

Serves: **4**

Preparation time: 10 minutes

Cooking time: 10 minutes

250 g/8 oz Chinese rice noodles
2 tablespoons vegetable oil
3–4 spring onions, sliced thinly diagonally
2.5 cm/1 inch piece fresh root ginger, finely chopped
1 clove garlic, crushed
2 skinless, boneless chicken breasts, each weighing about 150 g/5 oz cut into thin strips across the grain
125 g/4 oz mangetout
125 g/4 oz lean sliced cooked ham, shredded
75 g/3 oz bean sprouts
pepper
SAUCE
2 teaspoons cornflour
8 tablespoons Chicken Stock (see page 39) or water
2 tablespoons soy sauce
2 tablespoons Chinese rice wine or dry sherry
2 teaspoons sesame oil

1 Cook the rice noodles according to packet instructions. Meanwhile, prepare the sauce ingredients. Mix the cornflour with 2 tablespoons of the stock or water to a smooth paste, then stir in the remaining stock or water, the soy sauce, Chinese rice wine or sherry and the sesame oil. Set aside. Drain the noodles, rinse under cold water and set aside.

2 Preheat the wok. Add the oil, swirl it around the wok and heat over a moderate heat until hot. Add the spring onions, ginger and garlic and stir-fry for 1–2 minutes or until softened but not browned. Add the chicken, increase the heat to high and stir-fry for 3–4 minutes or until lightly coloured on all sides.

3 Add the mangetout and stir-fry for 1–2 minutes or until just tender, then add the ham and bean sprouts and stir-fry to mix. Stir the sauce, pour it into the wok and bring to the boil, stirring constantly. Add the drained noodles and toss until combined and piping hot. Season with pepper to taste and serve immediately.

Rice and Grains

Types of Grain

Long-grain Rice

Regular Long-grain White Rice

These slim, long grains have been milled to remove the husk and bran layers. This rice is suitable for most savoury dishes, especially many American, Mexican, Spanish and Caribbean recipes. It can also be used in Chinese recipes.

Regular Long-grain Brown Rice

A wholegrain rice, milled only enough to remove the outer husk, but still retaining the bran layer. This gives a distinctly nutty flavour and chewy texture. It can be used instead of white long-grain rice in most dishes.

Easy-cook Rice

This may be either white or brown and has been steamed under pressure before milling to harden the grain, ensuring that it keeps its shape well during cooking and that the grains stay separate. It is a good choice for salads and stir-fries.

Speciality Rice

Basmati Rice

This very long grain has a delicate aroma and flavour. It is an excellent choice for Indian dishes, such as pilau and biryani.

Camargue Red Rice

An unusual short-grain rice grown in the South of France. It has an attractive russet-red colour, with a nutty flavour and chewy texture, rather like brown rice.

Glutinous Rice

A round, pearly grain that becomes sticky when cooked and has a slightly sweet flavour. It is used to make some Chinese rice cakes and in similar dishes.

Jasmine Rice or Thai Fragrant Rice

This is another aromatic rice with a delicate flavour. The cooked grains combine a soft, slightly sticky outer texture with a firm bite. It is a good choice for Chinese and South-east Asian dishes.

Risotto Rice

This is a medium-grain rice, the main varieties being Arborio and Carnaroli, that absorbs up to five times its weight in liquid during cooking. Starch released from the grains during cooking gives classic risottos their characteristically creamy texture.

Pudding Rice

This is a short-grain rice that clings together

when cooked, making it an ideal choice for rice puddings and sweets.

Sushi Rice

Different varieties of Japanese rice are used for sushi and expert chefs have their favourite grain. Sushi rice grains remain separate and firm, but they cling together when cooked.

Other Grains

Barley, Pearl Barley, Oats, Rye, Wheat and Millet

These whole grains may all be added to stews and casseroles. Millet is particularly good with Indian and African dishes.

Buckwheat

This is in fact a seed. Roasted, buckwheat is also known as a kasha in Eastern European countries. It cooks quickly and can be served as an alternative to rice.

Bulgar Wheat

This is a cooked wheat that has been dried and lightly crushed. It should not be confused wiith cracked wheat, which is raw. Bulgar needs only soaking or light cooking before serving. It makes a deliciously nutty-flavoured accompaniment to savoury dishes and can be used as a base for salads.

Couscous

This is made from wheat semolina that is steamed and rolled to give a creamy-coloured grain-like product. It is now sold as an instant product, which requires short soaking, making it a quick and easy accompaniment for savoury dishes, particularly Moroccan-style stews. It is also a good base for salads.

Millet

Rich in iron and protein, these fine grains cook quickly to make excellent pilaf. Millet is also good in burgers.

Polenta

A fine, granular cornmeal that is a staple food in Italy. Polenta is very versatile and is often served with meat or vegetable dishes instead of pasta, rice or bread. It can be eaten cold or hot, in slices, either fried or grilled. Instant polenta is the most common type available, and it is very quick to cook.

Wild Rice

This is not actually a rice at all, but an aquatic grass that was a traditional food of the American Indians. It has a very firm texture and a full, nutty flavour. Mainly used in savoury dishes, it is often mixed with white rice in order to add a contrast of colour as well as texture and flavour.

Cooking Grains

Bulgar Wheat, Roasted Buckwheat or Millet

Place the grain in a saucepan and cover with about double its volume of boiling water. Bring to the boil, reduce the heat and cover the pan. Simmer gently for 10–15 minutes or until the grains are tender and all the water is absorbed.

Couscous

Put the couscous into a large heatproof bowl and pour in enough boiling water to cover it. Allow about 400 ml/14 fl oz to 250 g/8 oz couscous. Cover and leave to soak for about 20 minutes. If necessary, melt a little butter or heat a little oil in a large frying pan or saucepan over a low heat, then add the couscous and stir for 2–3 minutes to heat through. Take care not to cook the couscous once it has soaked or it will become very stodgy.

Polenta

Allow 1.5 litres/2½ pints water and 2 teaspoons salt to 300 g/10 oz instant polenta. Bring the water to the boil in a large saucepan. Add the salt and sprinkle in the polenta, stirring continuously to prevent lumps from forming. Bring to the boil, then simmer gently, stirring constantly, for 10–12 minutes, until the polenta begins to come away from the sides of the pan. Serve just as it is. Alternatively, grease a shallow tin and spread the polenta into it to a thickness of about 1.5 cm/¾ inch. Leave to set. To serve, cut into slices, brush with olive oil and grill until golden.

To Steam Grains

This method can be used for processed grains, such as bulgar wheat or couscous. Put the grains in a large bowl and cover with plenty of cold water. Leave to soak for 10 minutes, then drain. Line a steamer or metal colander with muslin and turn the grain into it. Place over a saucepan of boiling water, cover tightly and steam for about 20 minutes, stirring lightly with a fork occasionally, until the grains are tender and fluffy.

How to Cook Perfect Rice

It is not necessary to rinse regular rice before cooking, but basmati, glutinous and jasmine rice are best rinsed thoroughly to remove excess starch from the surface of the grains before cooking. Place the rice in a sieve and rinse under cold running water until the water runs clear. There are two main methods of cooking rice.

Absorption Method

Put 250 g/8 oz rice (4 servings) in a saucepan. Add the measured amount of cold water (see chart below) and bring to the boil. Stir once, then cover and reduce the heat to a gentle simmer. Cook for the recommended time, until the rice is tender and the water absorbed.

Free Simmer Method

Bring 1.5 litres/2½ pints water to the boil in a large saucepan. Add 250 g/8 oz rice, bring back to the boil and reduce the heat. Simmer, uncovered, for the recommended time, until the rice is tender. Drain well.

Adding Flavour to Plain Grains

Try one of the following simple methods of adding extra flavour when cooking rice or other grains.

Stock

Use a well-flavoured stock instead of water. Rice for sweet dishes may be cooked with fruit juices.

Coconut Milk

Rice cooked in coconut milk is very good with Thai dishes. Use the absorption method and use thin coconut milk instead of water.

Spices

Add a pinch of saffron strands to plain rice, risottos or couscous. Fry a few lightly crushed coriander seeds and/or cumin seeds in a little hot oil for about 1 minute, then stir into the cooked rice or grain.

Sesame

Add a light drizzle of sesame oil or a sprinkling of toasted sesame seeds to cooked rice for serving with oriental dishes.

Pesto

Stir a spoonful of Pesto alla Genovese (see page 37) into cooked rice or couscous to add a deliciously rich, Mediterranean flavour.

Tips for Perfect Risottos

1 For a classic, creamy-textured risotto, choose good-quality risotto rice such as Arborio or Carnaroli.

2 Add the rice to some hot butter or oil and stir to coat the grains thoroughly before adding any liquid.

3 If you are using wine, add this to the rice first and allow it to evaporate before adding the other liquid.

4 Add boiling stock gradually, a ladleful at a time, allowing each addition to be absorbed before adding the next.

5 Stir the risotto gently and continuously for 15–20 minutes, until the rice is tender with a slight firmness in the centre of the grain.

6 To avoid overcooking, remove the risotto from the heat a few minutes before you think it is cooked, since it will continue to cook in its own heat.

Type of Rice	Water Quantity	Cooking Time
	(Absorption method)	(both methods)
Regular long-grain	500 ml/17 fl oz	12 minutes
Easy-cook long grain	575 ml/18 fl oz	15 minutes
Regular brown long-grain	625 ml/21 fl oz	35 minutes
Easy-cook long-grain brown	650 ml/23 fl oz	30 minutes

Nutty Couscous and Rice Salad

Simple and quick, this mixed grain salad has a characteristically North African flavour with dried fruit, pine nuts, almonds and mint.

Serves: **4**

Preparation time: 10 minutes

Cooking time: 20 minutes

250 g/8 oz couscous
450 ml/¾ pint boiling water
175 g/6 oz long-grain rice
2 tablespoons olive oil
1 fresh red chilli, deseeded and finely chopped
1 garlic clove, crushed
125 g/4 oz blanched almonds, coarsely chopped
25 g/1 oz pine nuts
125 g/4 oz ready-to-eat dried apricots, coarsely chopped
25 g/1 oz raisins
6 tablespoons mixed chopped mint and parsley
DRESSING
150 ml/¼ pint olive oil
4 tablespoons mixed lemon juice and white wine vinegar
salt and pepper

1 Put the couscous into a bowl and pour the boiling water over it. Set the couscous aside to soak for about 20 minutes, until the water has been absorbed. Use a fork to fluff up the couscous occasionally.

2 Meanwhile, cook the rice in a large saucepan of boiling lightly salted water for 12–15 minutes until tender.

3 To make the dressing, whisk together the oil, lemon juice and vinegar, then season to taste with salt and pepper. Alternatively, put all the ingredients in a screw-top jar and shake vigorously.

4 Heat the olive oil in a heavy-based frying pan. Add the chilli, garlic, almonds and pine nuts. Cook, stirring occasionally, until the nuts have browned.

5 Drain the rice and transfer to a warmed serving bowl. Fluff it up with a fork, then add the couscous, the nut mixture, apricots, raisins, mint and parsley. Pour in the dressing and toss well to mix.

Red Wine Risotto

Field mushrooms belong to the same family as the cultivated variety but have a stronger flavour and are more aromatic. Other wild mushrooms, such as chanterelles or morels, would be equally delicious in this dish. For a truly authentic Italian flavour, you could use porcini mushrooms, which are also known as ceps or boletus.

Serves: **4**

Preparation time: 5 minutes

Cooking time: 20 minutes

600 ml/1 pint Chicken Stock (see page 39)
450 ml/¾ pint red wine
1 tablespoon extra virgin olive oil
125 g/4 oz butter
2 garlic cloves, crushed
2 red onions, chopped
300 g/10 oz Arborio or Carnaroli rice
250 g/8 oz field mushrooms, sliced
175 g/6 oz Parmesan cheese, freshly grated
salt and pepper

1 Heat the stock and red wine together in a large saucepan to a gentle simmer.

2 Heat the olive oil and 50 g/2 oz of the butter in a heavy-based saucepan. Add the garlic and onions and sauté over a low heat for 5 minutes, until softened, but not browned.

3 Add the rice and mix well to coat the grains with the butter and oil. Add enough of the hot stock to cover the rice, stir well and simmer gently. Continue to stir as frequently as possible throughout cooking. As the liquid is absorbed, add more stock, 1 ladle at a time, just to cover the rice, stirring well.

4 When half the stock has been incorporated, add the mushrooms and season to taste with salt and pepper. The rice should be stained with the colour of the wine, giving it a rich dark red colour.

5 When all the stock has been added, and the rice is just cooked with a good creamy sauce, add most of the Parmesan and the remaining butter and mix well. Transfer to a warm serving dish, garnish with the remaining Parmesan and serve with the rest of the bottle of red wine.

FOOD FACT • It is much better to buy Parmesan in a single piece and grate it freshly when required. Ready-grated cheese quickly loses its flavour and texture when stored.

Chocolate Rice Ramekins with Caramel

A creative, up-market variation on the traditional and ever-popular rice pudding, using chocolate and caramel. Use small ramekin dishes or individual metal pudding moulds to shape the puddings.

Serves: **6**

Preparation time: 20 minutes, plus cooling

Cooking time: about 1 hour

Oven temperature: 180°C/350°F/Gas Mark 4

150 g/5 oz pudding rice
450 ml/¾ pint milk
1 teaspoon vanilla essence
50 g/2 oz caster sugar
125 g/4 oz dark chocolate, chopped
3 egg yolks
150 ml/¼ pint double cream
CARAMEL
175 g/6 oz sugar
4 tablespoons water
single cream or Vanilla Sauce (see page 31) to
  serve (optional)

1 Put the rice, milk, vanilla essence and sugar in a heavy-based saucepan and bring to the boil. Reduce the heat, cover and simmer gently, stirring occasionally, for about 20 minutes, until the rice is just tender and most of the liquid has been absorbed.

2 Stir in 100 g/3½ oz of the chocolate until melted. Whisk the egg yolks with the cream and stir into the rice.

3 For the caramel, put the sugar in a small heavy-based saucepan, together with half the water. Heat very gently until the sugar dissolves. Bring to the boil and boil rapidly until the syrup has turned to a pale caramel colour. Stir in the remainder of the water (standing back as the caramel will splutter slightly) and cook until the caramel has softened again.

4 Pour the caramel into 6 small ramekins or metal moulds, tilting them so it coats the sides. Spoon in the rice mixture. Place the moulds in a roasting tin and pour in sufficient hot water to come halfway up the sides of the moulds. Bake in a preheated oven, 180°C/350°F/Gas Mark 4, for 20 minutes, until the rice is just set. Remove from the oven and set aside to cool.

5 Melt the remaining chocolate in a heatproof bowl set over a saucepan of barely simmering water. Trail lines of melted chocolate over 6 serving plates. Loosen the edges of the rice puddings with a knife, then invert them on to the plates. Serve with single cream or vanilla sauce, if liked.

Beans, Peas and Lentils

Pulses

Beans, peas and lentils are all pulses. They are economical, high in fibre and low in fat, and are a valuable source of vegetable protein, particularly in vegetarian diets.

Lentils

The most common types are red lentils, green or continental lentils and the smaller brown lentils. Puy lentils are a darker, green-grey colour. Any type of whole lentil can be used in soups, stews, bakes and pasta dishes; Puy lentils are especially good braised with rich meats and game. Whole lentils cook quite quickly without pre-soaking, but you can also buy cans of ready-cooked lentils to save time. Red, orange or yellow lentils are split and their husks have been removed. They cook quickly, becoming very soft. They do not remain firm and separate in the same way as whole lentils. They are useful for creamy dishes, such as Indian dhal, or for bulking out minced meat in

dishes such as cottage pie, and also make good stuffings or vegetarian burgers.

Beans

Dried beans are good storecupboard ingredients. It is best to buy small quantities, since old beans dry out and toughen with age. Canned beans are cooked and convenient, being ready to use.

Adzuki Beans

These are small and dark red, with a slightly sweet flavour. They can be used in place of lentils, since they cook quickly and have a mealy texture. They are also good for sprouting, such as mung beans (see page 79).

Black Beans

These glossy black-skinned beans are good in casseroles and soups. They can be used instead of red kidney beans.

Black-eye Beans

These cream-coloured beans have a small black ring on one side resembling an eye. They have a pleasant nutty flavour and can be used in soups, casseroles and salads.

Borlotti Beans

Also known as *rose coco* beans because of their rosy-speckled skins, these are popular in Italian dishes. They have a texture similar to red kidney beans and can be used in the same way as them.

Broad Beans

These have a fairly strong flavour and can be tough unless the outer skin is removed. They can be puréed with a little lemon juice and oil to make a delicious dip.

Cannellini Beans

These creamy white beans have a soft texture and they are very good hot or cold, in casseroles or salads. They are a favourite in Italian cooking.

Chick Peas

Versatile in all kinds of casseroles and salads, or served with couscous, chick peas can be mashed to make little savoury balls known as falafel or puréed to make hummus, a dip.

Haricot Beans

These versatile beans are best known in the form of canned baked beans. They take on other flavours well, so are ideal for casseroles and stews, particularly the classic cassoulet, a stew of mixed meats with beans.

Mung Beans

These small green beans are the traditional bean for sprouting, but they are also good in salads and stews. Without their skins, they are a golden yellow colour and are known as mung dhal in Indian cooking.

Pinto Beans

These speckled pale brown beans are a good substitute for red kidney beans.

Red Kidney Beans

The classic choice for Chilli con Carne (see pages 84–85) and Mexican refried beans. These popular beans are also used in Caribbean dishes.

Soya Beans

These versatile beans have a high protein content and quite a delicate flavour. Firm in texture, soya beans require long soaking and cooking. They can also be sprouted successfully, and the sprouted beans can be used in stir-fries and salads.

Butter Beans

Known as lima beans in America, these have a distinctive buttery-mealy texture and creamy colour. They are excellent served as a vegetable dish on their own with cream or butter and herbs.

Flageolet Beans

Long in shape and pale green in colour, these beans have a delicate flavour and are equally good hot or cold. The French traditionally serve them with lamb.

How To Cook Dried Pulses

Pre-Soaking Dried Pulses

There is no need to soak lentils, split peas and mung beans before cooking, but most other dried pulses are pre-soaked to reduce the cooking time.

Wash the beans in a large bowl of cold water, removing any grit or debris, then drain well in a sieve. Cover with fresh cold water to double their depth and leave to soak for 6–8 hours or overnight. Soya beans should be soaked for at least 24 hours or up to 2 days, changing the water daily. Drain and rinse the beans before cooking them.

If time is short, you can place the beans in a large saucepan, cover with water and bring to the boil. Boil for 1 minute, then remove from the heat and leave to soak for 1 hour. Drain and rinse before cooking.

Pre-Cooking Beans

Some types of beans should be boiled rapidly before cooking, since they contain an enzyme

Making Bean or Lentil Purées

Cooked or canned beans and lentils can be puréed quickly to make dips or side dishes.

1 Drain the beans and purée them in a blender or food processor, adding a little single cream or stock to moisten them to a soft consistency. Process until fairly smooth, but still retaining a little texture. Alternatively, rub the beans through a coarse sieve with the back of a wooden spoon. For a coarse purée, mash the beans with a fork, adding a little butter or cream to the hot beans to soften the texture.

2 Stir in a little crushed garlic, chopped fresh herbs or grated nutmeg and season with salt and pepper to taste. Serve warm as a side dish or cold as a dip with pitta bread or vegetable sticks, to dunk.

How to Grow Sprouts

It is very easy to sprout beans. The process takes only a few days, so you can always have a fresh supply of bean sprouts to use in salads or stir-fries. The best pulses to use are mung, aduki and soya beans, chick peas and whole lentils.

1 You will need about 4 tablespoons beans or lentils – they will increase in size to about 6 times their original volume, so this amount makes about 2 cupfuls of sprouts. Wash the beans, drain and cover with cold water, then soak overnight.

2 Drain and rinse the beans, then place in a large clean jar (a large coffee jar is ideal). Cover the top of the jar with a piece of muslin or fine cotton and secure it around the rim with a rubber band. Place the jar in a warm, dark place.

3 Rinse the beans with cold water 2–3 times a day, draining them through the muslin, for 3–4 days until you have crisp white bean sprouts. Packed with vitamins, they are ready to use.

---

that is not destroyed by simmering and may cause stomach upsets. These are red kidney, borlotti, aduki and black beans. Put the drained, soaked beans in a large saucepan, cover to double their depth with cold water and bring to a full boil. Boil hard for 10 minutes, then drain and cook as usual.

Cooking Beans and Pulses

Put the drained, soaked beans in a large saucepan and cover to at least double their depth with cold water. Bring to the boil, then reduce the heat and cover the pan. Simmer the beans until tender. Do not add salt until the beans are completely tender, since it prevents them from softening, and it will toughen part-cooked beans.

Cooking Times for Dried Pulses

Cooking times vary according to how long the dried beans have been stored. These standard times are a basic guide.

Whole lentils, split peas, mung and aduki beans	25–30 minutes
Lima, black-eye, flageolet beans, dried peas	40–45 minutes
Red kidney, cannellini, borlotti and black beans	1 hour
Pinto, butter and haricot beans, chick peas	1¼–1½ hours
Soya beans	3–4 hours

Warm Chick Pea Salad

Being firm in texture and nutty in flavour, chick peas make an ideal main ingredient for salads. Warming them in the dressing allows the chick peas to absorb all the flavours, and because they are firm in texture, there is no danger of their disintegrating in the process.

Serves: **4**

Preparation time: 5 minutes

Cooking time: about 10 minutes

5 tablespoons extra virgin olive oil
1 red onion, finely chopped
2 garlic cloves, crushed
4 cm/1½ inch piece of fresh root ginger, grated
2 x 400 g/13 oz cans chick peas, drained
pinch of dried chilli flakes
juice and finely grated rind of 1½ lemons
1 bunch of coriander, chopped
salt and pepper
mixed ground cumin and paprika, to garnish

1 Heat 1 tablespoon of the oil in a frying pan. Add the onion, garlic and ginger and cook gently for 5–7 minutes, stirring occasionally, until soft and translucent.

2 Add the chick peas, chilli flakes and lemon rind and stir for about 30 seconds, then add the lemon juice and let the mixture bubble until it is almost dry. Add the coriander and season to taste with salt and pepper.

3 Transfer the mixture to a serving dish, pour over the remaining olive oil and set aside to cool. Serve at room temperature, sprinkled with a little ground cumin and paprika.

FOOD FACT • Extra virgin olive oil is the best quality and, although rather expensive, its unique flavour is perfect for salad dressings. Virgin olive oil also has an excellent flavour and is a good oil for cooking. Olive oil that is labelled 'pure' has been refined and possibly heat-treated, and therefore lacks the special flavour of the other types of olive oil.

Italian Bean Casserole

Serves: **4**

Preparation time: 15 minutes, plus soaking

Cooking time: 1¾ hours

Oven temperature: 160°C/325°F/Gas Mark 3

125 g/4 oz red kidney beans, soaked in cold water overnight
125 g/4 oz cannellini beans, soaked in cold water overnight
125 g/4 oz flageolet beans, soaked in cold water overnight
2 tablespoons olive oil
1 onion, chopped
1 green pepper, deseeded and chopped
1 teaspoon dried oregano
150 g/5 oz can tomato purée
300 ml/½ pint water
1 teaspoon caster sugar
salt and pepper
oregano or marjoram sprigs, to garnish

1 Cook the beans separately to avoid the red beans colouring the others. Cover with cold water, bring to the boil, boil rapidly for 10 minutes, then reduce the heat and simmer until the beans are just cooked (see page 79).

2 Heat the oil in a heavy-based frying pan. Add the onion and green pepper and fry over a medium heat, stirring occasionally, for about 5 minutes, until softened.

3 Add the oregano, tomato purée, water and sugar, season to taste with salt and pepper and bring to the boil.

4 Drain the beans, put them into a casserole and pour the onion and pepper sauce over them. Cook, uncovered, in a preheated oven, 160°C/325°F/Gas Mark 3, stirring frequently but gently, for 1 hour, until most of the liquid has been absorbed.

5 Serve the bean casserole garnished with oregano or marjoram sprigs.

FOOD FACT • The beans can be cooked up to 1 day in advance. Keep covered and chilled.

Chilli con Carne

You can make this dish as hot or mild as you like by adjusting the amount of chilli powder. For a really fiery meal, serve with bottled or smoked chillies.

Serves: **4**

Preparation time: 5 minutes

Cooking time: 45 minutes

2 tablespoons vegetable oil
1 large red onion, sliced
1–2 garlic cloves, crushed
750 g/1½ lb minced beef
1 teaspoon hot chilli powder
½ teaspoon ground cumin
425 g/14 oz can tomatoes
150 ml/¼ pint beef stock
1 teaspoon caster sugar
2 tablespoons tomato purée
490 g/15½ oz can red kidney beans, drained
salt and pepper
flat-leafed parsley sprigs, to garnish
TO SERVE
250 g/8 oz long-grain rice, cooked (see page 67)
soured cream (optional)

1 Heat the oil in a flameproof casserole. Add the onion and garlic and fry over a medium heat, stirring occasionally, for 7 minutes, until golden. Add the minced beef, chilli powder and cumin and fry, stirring constantly, until the beef is well browned.

2 Stir in the tomatoes with their juice, the stock, sugar and tomato purée and season with salt and pepper to taste. Bring to the boil, then lower the heat, cover and simmer gently for 30 minutes.

3 Add the kidney beans 5 minutes before the end of cooking time. Adjust the seasoning to taste and garnish with parsley sprigs. Serve with long-grain rice and topped with a spoonful of soured cream, if liked.

VARIATION • Try adding 1 or 2 squares of plain chocolate instead of the sugar for a rich and unusual flavour.

Fish and Shellfish

Types of Fish and Shellfish

Fish

Fish are usually classified into three groups. Within each group, most types of fish are interchangeable in recipes. Generally speaking, white fish are best cooked by moist methods, such as poaching or steaming, or in sauces. Oily fish are good for grilling or roasting.

When choosing whole fish, look for bright, clear eyes and moist, shiny, firm scales. The gills should be bright red and the fish should have a clean, fresh fishy smell with no trace of ammonia.

White Fish

This group can be split according to the shape of the fish.

Round White Fish

This includes bass, catfish, coley, conger eel, haddock, hake, huss, grey mullet, gurnard, John Dory, ling, pollack, red mullet, sea bass, sea bream and whiting.

Large round white fish, such as cod or coley, are usually sold as fillets, steaks or cutlets. The smaller round fish, such as haddock or whiting, are usually sold as fillets.

Flat White Fish

This includes brill, dab, Dover sole, flounder, halibut, lemon sole, megrim, monkfish, plaice, skate and turbot. The larger flat fish, such as halibut or turbot, are usually sold as fillets or steaks, and sometimes whole. Smaller flat fish, such as plaice or sole, are usually sold as fillets or whole.

Oily Fish

This includes anchovy, brown trout, eel, herring, mackerel, pilchard, rainbow trout, salmon, sardines, sea trout, sprats, tuna and whitebait. Most small oily fish are sold whole, but rainbow trout and mackerel are often sold as fillets. Salmon can be bought whole or in fillets, steaks or cutlets. Tuna is usually available as steaks.

Exotic Fish

There is now an increasing array of more unusual fish available, imported from the warm waters of the Indian Ocean, the Caribbean and the New Zealand coasts. There is no need to be daunted by their exotic appearance, since these fish can be cooked by any of the methods used for familiar fish.

Look out for steaks of swordfish, shark and the highly prized marlin, all of which have a firm, meaty texture similar to tuna. These are ideal for barbecuing or grilling. Red snapper, silk snapper, red mullet, red sea bream, grouper,

telapia (St Peter's fish) and Spanish mackerel are examples of the many exotics now appearing regularly on our fish counters. They are usually sold whole, ready cleaned, and are excellent served on the bone, grilled, baked, poached or steamed.

Shellfish

These are divided into two main types.

Crustaceans

These shellfish have legs and they include crab, crawfish, crayfish, lobster, prawn, scampi and shrimps. These are mostly sold cooked. Before buying them, you should make sure the shells are intact. Lobster, crawfish and crab should feel heavy for their size and should have no free liquid inside – check by shaking the shellfish gently and listen for a tell-tale swishing sound.

Avoid buying very small lobsters since those weighing less than 500 g/1 lb provide very little flesh. An ideal weight is 750 g–1 kg/1½–2 lb. When buying crab, it is worth knowing that male crabs have more white meat because of their large front claws and females have the rich pink coral inside. So, choose the sex of your crab according to your taste.

Prawns and shrimps are usually sold ready cooked, and have often been pre-frozen. Cold water prawns from the icy waters of the North Atlantic always come ready cooked and ready to eat. Warm-water prawns vary in size, since there are many different varieties, but these are the best choice for stir-frying.

Raw prawns, particularly tiger prawns which are mainly imported from Thailand, are more readily available frozen, and these are a good choice for cooked dishes because they have a fresher flavour and are less likely to dry out

during cooking. Raw prawns come in their shells, often with the head already removed, or ready peeled, often with the tail tip left on for decoration.

Molluscs

These are shellfish without legs and they include cockles, clams, mussels, oysters, scallops, squid, whelks and winkles. When choosing any molluscs, look for those with clean, tightly closed, undamaged shells. Clams, oysters and scallops are still alive when you buy them fresh in closed shells, so avoid any with open shells that do not close when tapped since this may indicate that they are not fresh. Scallops sold out of shell or on the half-shell should be creamy ivory in colour,

with a bright, orange coral. Avoid any that are very white in colour, as they may have been soaked in water to add to the weight and plump up their appearance. Small queens are round nuggets of white flesh without corals.

Cockles are usually sold ready cooked and shelled, often in vinegar or brine, but if you do buy them live in closed shells, treat them as for mussels (see page 97). Wash them well in several changes of cold water since they can be gritty if any sand remains in the shell.

How to Prepare Fish

Removing Fish Scales

This is known as scaling or descaling. Hold the fish under running water or over a sheet of newspaper. Holding the tail, draw the back of a knife firmly down the fish from head to tail, scraping off the scales. Rinse the fish under cold water and dry on kitchen paper.

Boning Whole Round Fish

This method is suitable for small fish, such as herring, mackerel or trout. Cut off the head, tail and fins. Slit the fish along the belly side, where it has been cleaned, and place it skin side uppermost on a board. Using your thumbs, press down firmly along the backbone of the fish, to release the bone from the flesh. Turn the fish over and lift out the bone, easing it off with a knife if necessary. Any fine bones that are left may be removed with tweezers.

Filleting Flat Fish

Lay the fish flat on a board. Cut a line down the backbone along the centre of the fish, from the head to the tail. Starting at the head end, insert the knife under the flesh, between it and the bones. Using long strokes, slide the knife between the flesh and bones. Keep the blade flat against the bones and work towards the outer edge, turning back the loosened fillet as you go. Remove the fillet on the other side of the fish, then turn the fish over to remove the two remaining fillets on the underside.

Oily fish fillets, such as mackerel, herring or trout, are excellent coated in oatmeal or rolled oats instead of flour before frying.

Cooking Fish in a Parcel or *en Papillote*

This simple method is the perfect way to keep fillets, cutlets or small whole fish really moist and tasty during cooking. All the flavour and aroma are sealed in until the fish is served and the parcels are opened at the table.

Cut a double-thick square of greaseproof paper or foil large enough to enclose the fish completely and brush it with melted butter or oil. Place the fish on top and sprinkle with salt, pepper and chopped herbs. If you like, tuck in some lemon slices or add a splash of dry white wine. Bring the sides of the foil or paper over the fish and fold the ends over firmly to seal in the fish and prevent the juices from escaping. Place on a baking sheet and cook in a preheated oven at 200°C/400°F/Gas Mark 6. Allow 10 minutes for thin fillets or 15 minutes if the fish is more than 2.5 cm/1 inch thick. Large whole fish, such as salmon, can be cooked in the same way allowing 15 minutes per 500 g/1 lb at 180°C/350°F/Gas Mark 4.

Tips for Cooking Perfect Fish

1 Cook only very fresh fish – if possible, buy the fish on the day you plan to cook it.

2 Most fish cooks quickly and dries out if cooked for too long, so take care not to overcook it.

3 To test whether fish is cooked, insert the point of a knife into the thickest part of the flesh: it should flake apart and lift away from the bone easily. Cooked fish should be opaque right through.

4 Serve fish as soon as it is cooked – if it is kept hot it will soon dry out, toughen and lose its flavour.

Filleting Round Fish

Holding the fish firmly, cut through behind the gills on one side to separate the fillet from the head. Cut along and into the backbone, from tail to head, then slide the knife between the flesh of the top fillet and bones. Lift the fillet gently away from the bones as you release it from the backbone. Turn the fish over and remove the fillet on the other side.

Skinning Fish Fillets

Place the fillet skin side down on a board with the tail end towards you. Dip your fingers in salt to give a good grip then hold the tail end of the fillet. Use the tip of the knife to separate the flesh from the skin at the tail end. Grasp the skin firmly, then hold the knife at a slight angle so that it is almost parallel to the fish skin, and slide it between the skin and flesh. Use a sawing action to cut the flesh off the skin and fold it back as you go.

Coating Fish Fillets with Flour

When shallow-frying fish fillets, a simple flour coating will keep the juices in and prevent the flesh of the fish from breaking up during the cooking process.

Sprinkle a shallow layer of plain or wholemeal flour on to a large plate and season it with salt and pepper. Pour a shallow covering of milk into a wide dish. Wash the fish and dry it on kitchen paper. Dip the fillets into the milk, turning to moisten both sides evenly, then drain off the excess before dipping into the flour. Press and turn to coat the other side.

Fish Plaki

Plakis are a feature of both Turkish and Greek cuisines, but typically in Turkey the fish is cut into steaks or pieces and it may be served cold, whereas the fish in a Greek plaki is cooked whole. Lemon is also characteristic of the Greek version.

Serves: **4**

Preparation time: 8–10 minutes

Cooking time: 1 hour

Oven temperature: 190°C/375°F/Gas Mark 5

approximately 1.25 kg/2½ lb fish, such as whole
  bass or grey mullet
1 large lemon
2 tablespoons virgin olive oil
1 onion, chopped
1 carrot, finely chopped
2 garlic cloves, chopped
1 teaspoon coriander seeds, crushed
500 g/1 lb ripe tomatoes, skinned, deseeded
  and chopped (see page 142)
3 halves of sun-dried tomato, chopped
75 ml/3 fl oz medium-bodied dry white wine
bunch of parsley, finely chopped
salt and pepper
flat-leafed parsley sprig, to garnish

1 Put the fish into an ovenproof dish. Squeeze the juice from half the lemon and pour it over the fish.

2 Heat the olive oil in a saucepan. Add the onion and carrot and cook, stirring occasionally, until the onion has softened but not coloured. Stir in the chopped garlic and cook for about 3 minutes.

3 Stir in the coriander seeds, tomatoes, sun-dried tomatoes, wine and parsley and season to taste with salt and pepper. Lower the heat and simmer for a few minutes, until well blended. Using a fish slice, lift the fish and pour about a quarter of the tomato mixture underneath. Lay the fish down again. Pour over the remaining tomato mixture. Thinly slice the remaining lemon half and lay the slices on top of the fish.

4 Cover the dish and bake in a preheated oven, 190°C/375°F/Gas Mark 5, for about 40 minutes, until the fish flakes when tested with the point of a sharp knife (see page 91). Garnish with a parsley sprig and serve.

Baked Cod Steaks with Mozzarella and Tomato Sauce

You could use any firm-fleshed white fish for this dish. Haddock is a good, everyday substitute for cod. For an exotic touch you could try shark steaks, and for a special occasion use halibut.

Serves: **4**

Preparation time: 7 minutes, plus cooling

Cooking time: 1 hour 20 minutes

Oven temperature: 200°C/400°F/Gas Mark 6

400 g/13 oz can chopped tomatoes
1 garlic clove, crushed
2 tablespoons olive oil, plus extra for brushing
1 teaspoon chopped thyme
1 teaspoon grated lemon rind
pinch of sugar
salt and pepper
2 tablespoons chopped basil
4 x 175 g/6 oz cod steaks, washed and dried
50 g/2 oz pitted black olives
250 g/8 oz mozzarella cheese, thinly sliced
basil sprigs, to garnish

1 Place the tomatoes, garlic, olive oil, thyme, lemon rind, sugar and seasoning in a small saucepan. Bring to the boil over a low heat, cover and simmer for 30 minutes. Remove the lid and cook for a further 15 minutes, until the sauce is thick. Stir in the basil and set aside to cool.

2 Place the cod steaks in a shallow, oiled ovenproof dish. Pour over the tomato sauce and scatter over the olives. Finally place the slices of cheese over the fish to cover them completely.

3 Cover the dish loosely with foil and bake in a preheated oven, 200°C/400°F/Gas Mark 6, for 20 minutes. Remove the foil and bake for a further 10–15 minutes, until the cheese is bubbling and golden and the fish is cooked through. Garnish with basil sprigs and serve immediately with a tomato and fresh basil salad and fresh bread, if liked.

How to Prepare Shellfish

Preparing Scallops

If the scallops are in their shells, slide a knife between the top and bottom shells and twist apart, cutting the muscle which attaches the scallop to the shell. Discard the flat shell. Pull off the grey frill and black intestinal thread that runs from the central white muscle to the base of the coral tongue. If the scallops are large, separate the coral from the white muscle and slice the white part into rounds.

Preparing Squid

Wash the squid well in cold water. Holding the body in one hand, pull off the head and tentacles. Feel inside the body pouch and pull out the pen or quill (a long piece of cartilage that looks like a semi-transparent stick) and the ink sac, if not already removed with the head parts. Unless the ink is needed for the recipe, both of these can be discarded. Rub off and pull away the mottled membrane covering the body pouch. Remove and discard the mouth from the centre of the cluster of tentacles. Small squid may be left whole, or

Opening (Shucking) Oysters

An oyster knife is the ideal tool for this, but it is not essential, since any short, strong, thick-bladed knife will do the job. Hold the oyster in a clean tea towel to protect your hand, with the rounded side underneath and the flatter shell on top. Holding firmly, carefully push the knife point firmly through the hinge between the two sides of the shell. Slide the knife blade to and fro, twisting it slightly to break the hinge. Lift off the top part of the shell, taking care not to spill the juices retained in the lower shell.

curved back of the prawn, then use the tip of the knife to scrape out the black vein.

Butterflying Prawns

Peel large prawns, leaving the tail on. Use a sharp knife to cut a deep slit down the underside, from head to tail, cutting almost through to the other side, but leaving the two halves attached. Place the prawns, cut side down, on a board and press flat to open them out into a butterfly shape. Dip into lightly whisked egg white, then into cornflour, shaking off any excess. Deep-fry in hot oil until golden, then serve hot, with a dip or soy sauce.

larger ones sliced into rings or strips. Cut up the tentacles.

Cleaning Mussels

Place the mussels in a bowl of cold water, then scrub under running water with a stiff brush to remove any dirt. Scrape off any barnacles with a knife and pull off the hairy 'beard' protruding from the edge of the shell. Rinse well. Discard any damaged mussels or any open mussels that do not close when tapped.

Cooking Mussels

1 Heat about 150 ml/¼ pint dry white wine, Fish or Vegetable Stock (see page 39), or water in a large saucepan with a few sprigs of parsley and slices of onion for flavour.

2 When the liquid boils, tip in the mussels and cover the pan with a tight-fitting lid.
3 Cook for 3–4 minutes, shaking the pan occasionally, until the mussels open.
4 Use a slotted spoon to remove the mussels from the pan and discard any shells that have not opened during cooking.

Preparing Prawns

To peel either raw or cooked prawns, grip the head between finger and thumb, and pinch it firmly to pull it away from the body. Grip the legs and pull them away. Peel off the shell. You can leave the tip of the tail in place if required.

The dark intestinal vein in large prawns, such as tiger prawns, has a bitter flavour, so remove before cooking. Make a shallow cut along the

Paella

Strictly speaking, the word paella refers to the heavy cast-iron pan in which this dish is traditionally cooked. There are as many paella recipes as there are cooks in Spain, and this combination of chicken and seafood is typical of the region of Valencia.

Serves: **4**

Preparation time: 15 minutes

Cooking time: 35–40 minutes

4 skinless, boneless chicken thighs
2 garlic cloves, crushed
1 onion, chopped
½ red pepper, deseeded and chopped
1 tablespoon olive oil
250 g/8 oz risotto rice (Arborio or Carnaroli)
125 g/4 oz squid, cleaned and sliced into rings (see page 96)
pinch of saffron strands
600 ml/1 pint Fish, Vegetable or Chicken Stock (see page 39)
1 bay leaf
250 g/8 oz fresh mussels in their shells, scrubbed and cleaned (see page 97)
50 g/2 oz peeled raw prawns (see page 97)
50 g/2 oz unpeeled raw prawns
50 g/4 oz frozen petit pois
sea salt and pepper
chopped parsley, to garnish

1 Place the chicken, garlic, onion and red pepper in a paella pan or a heavy-based frying pan, together with the oil. Fry over a medium heat for about 10 minutes, turning the chicken so that it is golden all over.

2 Add the rice and squid and continue cooking for 5 minutes, until the rice starts to turn opaque. Stir in the saffron and pour over the stock. Add the bay leaf.

3 Add the shellfish to the rice mixture and lower the heat to a gentle simmer. Cook, without stirring, for 20–25 minutes, until the rice is tender and the stock absorbed. About 5 minutes from the end of the cooking time, add the peas. Stir occasionally. Season to taste with salt and pepper, sprinkle with chopped parsley and serve immediately.

Scallop, Prawn and Parma Ham Kebabs

A classic combination of scallops with Parma ham is glazed with sun-dried tomato paste as it cooks. This paste is available commercially or you can simply purée a few sun-dried tomatoes with some of the oil from the jar. You will need 4 skewers; if they are wooden, soak them for 30 minutes before use to prevent charring. Cook the kebabs on the barbecue or under a conventional grill.

Serves: **4**

Preparation time: 15 minutes, plus marinating

Cooking time: 6–8 minutes

4 thick slices of Parma ham, cut lengthways into 3 strips
12 large fresh scallops, cleaned, washed and dried (see page 96)
12 raw tiger prawns, washed and dried
6 tablespoons olive oil
1½ tablespoons sun-dried tomato paste
lemon wedges, to serve

MARINADE
125 ml/4 fl oz olive oil, plus extra for brushing
2 garlic cloves, minced
grated rind of 1 lemon
1 teaspoon ground coriander
1 teaspoon paprika
¼ teaspoon chilli powder
4½ teaspoons sun-dried tomato paste

MANGO SALSA
½ small ripe mango, peeled, pitted and diced
1 tablespoon chopped red onion
1 tablespoon chopped coriander
1 small fresh red chilli, deseeded and chopped
1 tablespoon dark soy sauce
1 tablespoon lime juice
1 teaspoon clear honey
salt and pepper

1 First, prepare the kebabs. Wrap each strip of ham around a scallop. Thread 3 prawns and 3 scallops alternately on to 4 skewers and place in a non-metallic dish.

2 Combine all the marinade ingredients, except the sun-dried tomato paste, and pour into the dish. Cover and set aside to marinate for at least 1 hour, or longer if possible.

3 Meanwhile, make the salsa. Put all the ingredients in a serving bowl, mix thoroughly and season with salt and pepper to taste. Chill in the refrigerator until required.

4 Remove the kebabs from the marinade. Beat the sun-dried tomato paste into the marinade, then brush the mixture over the scallops and prawns. Brush the barbecue grid or the rack of a grill pan with a little oil to prevent the kebabs from sticking and cook them, turning and brushing with the marinade frequently, for 6–8 minutes, until lightly charred and tender. Serve at once with lemon wedges and the mango salsa.

Prawns in Chillied Tomato Sauce

The prawns for this recipe should be firm, fresh and full of flavour, so do not use the small frozen ones that ooze water when cooked or you will have a disappointing dish.

Serves: **4**

Preparation time: 10 minutes

Cooking time: 10–12 minutes

2 tablespoons olive oil

2 red onions, finely chopped

3 garlic cloves, crushed

1 fresh red chilli, deseeded and chopped

2 strips of lemon rind

2 large, ripe, well-flavoured ridged tomatoes, deseeded and chopped

150 ml/¼ pint Fish Stock (see page 39)

500 g/1 lb raw peeled tiger prawns (see page 97)

salt and pepper

2 tablespoons chopped mixed parsley and dill

1 Heat the oil in a heavy-based frying pan. Add the onions, garlic, chilli and lemon rind and fry over a medium heat, stirring occasionally, for 1–2 minutes. Add the tomatoes and fish stock and bring to the boil. Lower the heat and simmer for 5 minutes.

2 Add the prawns, season to taste with salt and pepper and cook, turning occasionally, for about 4 minutes, until the prawns change colour. Sprinkle with the mixed herbs and serve immediately.

FOOD FACT • The heads, tails and shells of prawns can be used to make a delicate but surprisingly flavoursome shellfish stock. Lightly pound them in a mortar and then bring them to the boil with the juice of ½ lemon and 150 ml/¼ pint white wine. Add 1.2 litres/2 pints water, 1 diced onion, 1 garlic clove, 3–4 parsley stalks and 2–3 whole black peppercorns. Simmer for about 15 minutes, strain and use.

Poultry and Game

Types of Poultry and Game

The term poultry covers domestic birds that are reared for the table, so it includes chicken, turkey, guinea fowl, duck and goose. Game refers to wild birds and animals that are hunted for food, including grouse, pheasant, partridge, quail, wild duck and wood pigeon. Deer, hare and rabbit are also game animals. However, many types of game that used only to be available wild are now farmed, particularly pheasant, quail, rabbit and venison (from deer).

Chicken

Chickens are sold oven-ready, either fresh or frozen, with or without giblets. The weight range is about 1.5–3.2 kg/3–7 lb. The giblets, when packed with the bird, are usually placed in a bag in the body cavity. They include the neck and offal (such as heart, liver and gizzard). If the bird is sold with giblets, remember to remove them before cooking.

Corn-fed Chickens

These are fed on maize, which gives them their characteristic yellow skin and yellow-tinted flesh, with a rich flavour. They are cooked in the same way as ordinary chicken.

Poussins

These are 4–6-week-old chickens, weighing 500-750 g/1–1½ lb. They are very tender and ideal for roasting or, if spatchcocked, they can be grilled or barbecued.

Chicken Portions

Boned or part-boned, with or without skin, these are convenient for a wide variety of cooking. Chicken quarters include drumstick and thigh or wing and breast. They are useful single portions for braising or roasting. Smaller joints, including drumsticks, thighs, breasts and wings, can be braised, grilled and fried. Stir-fry strips and minced chicken are also available.

Free-range Chicken

By law, this now covers the following categories of chicken.
Free-range: Reared in specially designed houses, the birds are allowed to roam in open-air runs (with at least 1 square metre per bird) for at least half their lifetime. Their diet must include at least 70% cereals.
Traditional Free-range: These birds come from breeds that thrive outdoors and have a slow growth rate. They have daytime access to open-air runs with at least 2 square metres per bird. Their diet must be at least 70% cereals.
Free-range Total Freedom: These have the same growing standards as Traditional Free-range, but they must also have continuous outside access without being fenced in runs.

Turkey

Oven-ready turkeys are available fresh or frozen, weighing between 2.3–9 kg/5–20 lb; larger birds are less widely available. Free-range, bronze turkeys are very fine in flavour.

Turkey Portions

The wide variety of portions allow turkey to be cooked by many methods. These include breast fillets and steaks, stir-fry strips, diced thigh meat, mince and boned and rolled joints.

Other Poultry

Guinea Fowl

These are sold at about 1.5 kg/3 lb in weight and can be cooked in the same way as chicken or pheasant. Guinea fowl has a fine, slightly gamey flavour.

Duckling

Oven-ready birds weigh 1.5–2.7 kg/3–6 lb. Duck has a higher proportion of fat and bone to meat than chicken or turkey, so allow about 500 g/1 lb per portion. Farmed duck is now reared to be leaner than traditional birds and wild duck has a lower proportion of meat (with more fat), so you should usually allow 1 wild duck for 2 people. Boneless breasts, with or without skin, and breast fillets weigh around 250–375 g/8–12 oz, and will serve 1–2 people. They are best grilled or baked. Duck quarters are also available.

Goose

This is still seasonal (geese do not respond well to intensive farming methods) and at its best from September to January. Frozen birds can be bought all year round. The birds weigh 3.6–6.3 kg/8–14 lb. Like duck, goose is rich in fat and yields a small proportion of meat, so a 3.6–4.5 kg/8–10 lb bird will serve just 6–8.

Game

Pheasant

Available both farmed and wild – the flavour of farmed birds is usually milder than that of wild. One bird serves 1–2 people. Young pheasants and hen (female) birds can be cooked in the same way as chicken and are good roasted; older birds and cocks are best casseroled, since the flesh can be tougher and drier.

Partridge

These small game birds usually provide 1 serving each, but older, larger birds may serve 2. They are best pot-roasted or braised since they can be dry if roasted without liquid.

Grouse

Small game birds, each serving 1–2. While young birds can be roasted, older birds need long, slow stewing to tenderise their flesh.

Quail

Wild quail are now a protected species and farmed birds are readily available throughout the year. Allow 2 per person for a main course.

They are good roasted, casseroled or spatchcocked (see page 108) and grilled.

Wood Pigeon
Small birds, best casseroled or braised, allowing 1 per person unless very large.

Hare and Rabbit
Rabbit is mainly farmed. Wild rabbit is available from local butchers. Both are mild-flavoured, pale meats which can be braised, casseroled, roasted, grilled or fried. Hare is quite different. It is a dark, full-flavoured meat that requires moist cooking methods for best results, although it can be slow-roasted.

Venison
Venison comes from various deer of different breeds and ages, male or female. The seasons for wild deer vary according to the particular animals. Farmed deer are now producing the majority of venison available in the supermarkets. This meat is suitable for roasting, braising or stewing according to the cut. It is sold as joints, steaks, cubed or minced. Similar to beef but slightly stronger and richer in flavour, venison can be very dry if overcooked, and requires moist cooking or marinating and basting. Use it instead of beef in casseroles, meatloaves and pies.

How to Prepare Poultry

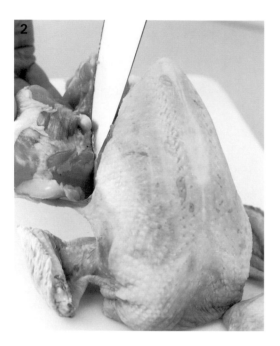

5 Place the breast half of the carcass skin upwards. Cut in half along the backbone, cutting close to the bone from the ridge of the breast and down through one side. Repeat on the second side, giving 2 portions each with breast and wing. Cut each portion in half again across the middle just behind the wing to separate the breast meat from the wing.

Spatchcocking

This is used for small and medium birds, such as poussin, small chickens, pheasant or guinea fowl, so that they lie flat and can be grilled, barbecued or roasted quickly and evenly.

1 With the bird breast side down, use a strong knife or poultry shears to cut through the flesh

Jointing

Jointing a whole bird is not as difficult as you may think. You will need a strong cook's knife or poultry shears.

1 Place the bird breast side up on a board and cut off the wing tips at the last joint.
2 To remove the leg and thigh in one portion, pull the leg away from the body and slice through the skin and flesh where the thigh joins the body. Cut through the ball and socket joint at the base of the thigh. Repeat to remove the other leg.
3 Divide each leg portion in 2 by cutting through the joint between the drumstick and the thigh.
4 Hold the chicken upright with the neck end downwards. Cut down firmly widthways through the body, separating the top, breast side (and wings) from the underside of the body. When you have cut through the ribs, pull the top and underside of the carcass apart. The bony underside of the carcass can be used for making stock.

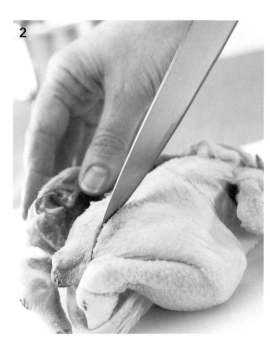

and ribs to one side of the backbone.

2 Cut down the other side of the backbone, then remove and discard it. Remove the small wishbone at the neck end.

3 Turn the bird over, breast side up. To open out and flatten the bird, press firmly on the breastbone with the heel of your hand.

4 To keep the bird flat and turn it easily during cooking, thread 2 wooden or metal skewers across through the bird. Push the first through a wing on one side and out through the thickest part of the thigh on the other side. Push the second skewer through parallel to the first towards the other end of the bird.

Skinning Portions

Much of the fat in poultry is in and directly under the skin, so if you remove the skin, the fat level (and the saturated fat level) will be considerably reduced. To remove the skin from joints, use the point of a knife to loosen it. Grasp the skin with a piece of kitchen paper to give a firm grip, and pull it away.

Flattening Breast Fillets

1 Place a boneless, skinless breast fillet between 2 large sheets of non-stick baking paper or clingfilm.

2 Use the side of a rolling pin or smooth meat hammer to beat the breast firmly all over the surface, flattening it as evenly as possible.

3 Remove the paper or film. The beaten-out poultry breast is ready for stuffing and rolling or for coating with egg and breadcrumbs before shallow-frying.

Stuffing Whole Birds

It is best to stuff large whole birds only at the neck end. Stuffing the body cavity creates a dense area of food that slows down the heat penetration and can prevent thorough cooking. Cook spare stuffing in a separate dish or roll it into balls to cook alongside the bird.

Before stuffing, make sure that the bird and stuffing are both at room temperature. Lift the neck flap of skin, loosening it gently from the

meat with your fingers. Use a small, sharp knife to cut out the 'V'-shaped wishbone just below the surface of the flesh.

Spoon the stuffing into the neck cavity. Do not overfill the cavity since the stuffing will expand and if it is packed in too tightly it may burst out during cooking. Smooth the skin back over the stuffing and tuck it underneath the bird to hold the stuffing in place.

Always weigh the bird after stuffing it to calculate the roasting time. Cook the bird promptly once stuffed – within 15 minutes – or refrigerate immediately until ready to cook.

Stuffing the Breast

Instead of stuffing the body cavity, loosen the skin from the meat at the vent end of the breast (use the point of a knife to start), then slide a spoon or your finger between the skin and meat all over the breast to create a large pocket. Fill with stuffing, butter or herbs and butter, spreading it out evenly under the skin.

Stuffing a Poultry Breast

1 Place the breast skin (or skinned) side uppermost on a board. Use a sharp knife to cut a slit horizontally into the side of the breast. Slice into the flesh, cutting parallel with the board, to make a deep pocket. Take care not to cut all the way through.

2 Use a small spoon to fill the pocket with stuffing – ricotta cheese flavoured with pesto makes a change from traditional stuffings. Alternatively, tuck in sprigs of herbs, ready-soaked dried apricots, prunes or diced mozzarella cheese. Take care not to overfill the pocket.

3 Secure the opening with a wooden cocktail stick or wrap a rasher of streaky bacon or a slice of Parma ham around the breast to keep the stuffing in place.

Scoring Duck Skin

When preparing duck breasts for grilling or frying with the skin on, use a sharp knife to score the skin deeply with lines or a diamond pattern to allow the fat to run out evenly. When cooking fatty duck breasts, start under or over a high heat and cook until the skin is golden brown, then turn over and reduce the heat to finish cooking. Drain well on kitchen paper.

Cooking Poultry and Game

Marinating

Marinating moistens and flavours foods, particularly dry poultry and game, prior to grilling or roasting. The marinade can be a simple mixture of olive oil and lemon juice, but it is also an opportunity to add a delicious sauce, coating or glaze.

Arrange the joints or portions in a large dish, preferably in a single layer. Mix the marinade ingredients thoroughly and pour over the poultry. Turn the pieces to coat them evenly, then cover with clingfilm and leave in the refrigerator to marinate for at least 30 minutes. Depending on the ingredients and the result required, marinating can take from minutes to hours or even 1–2 days.

Drain off the excess marinade before cooking, reserving it to baste the meat or to make a sauce. Any of the following mixtures can be used for grilled or barbecued poultry.

Herb and Lemon

4 tablespoons dry white wine
4 tablespoons olive oil
finely grated rind and juice ½ lemon
2 tablespoons finely chopped fresh herbs, such as parsley, thyme and chives
freshly ground pepper

Honey and Soy Sauce

3 tablespoons sunflower oil
2 tablespoons clear honey
1 tablespoon soy sauce
3 tablespoons orange juice
1 teaspoon prepared English mustard

Devilled Marinade

3 tablespoons sunflower oil
3 tablespoons Worcestershire sauce
3 tablespoons tomato purée
2 tablespoons lime or lemon juice

Spiced Yogurt

150 ml/¼ pint natural yogurt
1 small onion, minced
1 garlic clove, crushed
1 teaspoon grated fresh root ginger
1 teaspoon ground coriander
1 teaspoon ground turmeric
½ teaspoon turmeric

Frying Poultry

Coating Portions for Frying

Coating portions helps to seal in flavour and juices, and prevents low-fat cuts from becoming dry. It can also be a good way of adding extra flavour.

Freshly made fine breadcrumbs (from white or brown bread) make a good coating, but they do not have to be plain – try stirring in curry spices, chopped herbs, finely chopped nuts or sesame seeds. For a different texture, use

freshly grated coconut, desiccated coconut or rolled oats. Dip the portions into flour and then into beaten egg before turning them in the mixture to coat them evenly. Brush the poultry with melted butter or oil and turn the pieces in a mixture of dry spices until evenly coated. To do this easily with the minimum of mess, put the spices in a large polythene bag, add the poultry pieces and hold the bag closed while tossing the poultry in the spices.

Dry-spice Coatings for Frying

These are useful for flavouring chicken or turkey before grilling or barbecuing.

Hot Cajun Spice Mix

2 teaspoons garlic salt
2 teaspoons freshly ground black pepper
1½ teaspoons paprika
1½ teaspoons ground cumin
1 teaspoon cayenne pepper

Roasting

For successful roasting, avoid trussing the bird too tightly, since this can prevent even cooking. In most cases, it is enough to tie the ends of the drumsticks together to hold the bird in shape. The top of the breast can be covered with streaky bacon to keep it moist during cooking. Alternatively, it can be smeared with butter and covered loosely with foil or basted regularly during cooking. For large birds that require lengthy cooking, such as turkey, the breast should be covered with foil once it has browned to prevent it from overcooking and drying out. The foil may be removed for the final 15–30 minutes to crisp the skin.

To allow fat to drain away easily from fatty poultry, such as duck or goose, prick the skin with a fork or skewer, penetrating through to the flesh. This allows the fat directly under the skin to run out as it melts during roasting. Always roast fatty birds on a rack in a deep roasting tin to raise the bird above the fat, which collects during cooking. Pour off the fat occasionally, especially when roasting goose.

Poultry and Game	Time	Temperature
Chicken	20 mins per 500 g/1 lb + 20 mins	190°C/375°F/Gas Mark 5
Duckling	15 mins per 500 g/1 lb + 15 mins	200°C/400°F/Gas Mark 6
Goose	15 mins per 500 g/1 lb + 15 mins	200°C/400°F/Gas Mark 6
Guinea Fowl	20 mins per 500 g/1 lb + 20 mins	190°C/375°F/Gas Mark 5
Poussins	45–60 mins (depending on size)	190°C/375°F/Gas Mark 5
Pheasant	about 50 minutes	200°C/400°F/Gas Mark 6
Partridge	about 40 minutes	200°C/400°F/Gas Mark 6

Turkey Roasting Times
(at 190°C/375°F/Gas Mark 5)

1.5–2.3 kg/3–5 lb	1½–1¾ hours
2.7 kg–3.2 kg/6–7 lb	1¾–2hours
3.6–4 kg/8–9 lb	2–2½ hours
4.5–5 kg/10–11lb	2¼–2¾hours
5.4 kg–5.9 kg/12–13 lb	2¾–3hours
6.3–6.8 kg/14–17 lb	3¼–3½ hours
8.2–10 kg/18–22 lb	3½–3¾hours

Checking if Poultry is Cooked

All poultry should be cooked thoroughly to avoid any risk of contamination and food poisoning. Use a fork or metal skewer to pierce the meat deeply through the thickest part of the flesh – usually the thigh area of a whole bird. When you pull out the fork, press gently and the juices that run out should be clear, not pink. If there is any trace of pink, the meat is not thoroughly cooked.

Carving Chicken or Turkey

The only essential tools are a sharp knife and a carving fork to hold the bird safely in position.

1 Once the bird is roasted, remove it from the oven and leave it in a warm place to 'rest' for about 15 minutes. This allows the meat time to become slightly firm and easier to carve.
2 Place the bird breast uppermost on a board and remove any trussing string or skewers.
3 Lift one end of a drumstick and use it to pull the whole leg away from the body, then cut through the joint between the thigh and the body.
4 Cut the leg in half at the joint to separate the thigh and drumstick. If large, the meat can be carved off in slices.
5 Cut down through the corner of the breast where the wing joins the body, cutting off the wing with some of the adjoining breast meat.
6 Continue slicing the meat down into slices on one side of the breast, working back from the wing end. Repeat the process on the other side of the bird.

Carving Duck and Goose

1 Place the bird breast side up on a board. Lift one end of a drumstick and use it to pull the whole leg away from the body, then cut through the joint between the thigh and the body. Serve the leg portions whole.
2 Cut down through the corner of the breast next to the wing, cutting through the joint to separate the wing from the body.
3 Cut off the meat down the length of one side of the body, carving it vertically in long, narrow slices.
4 Repeat the process on the other side of the bird.

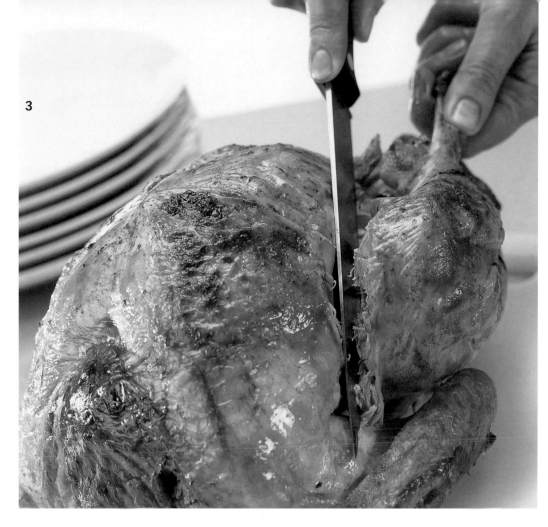

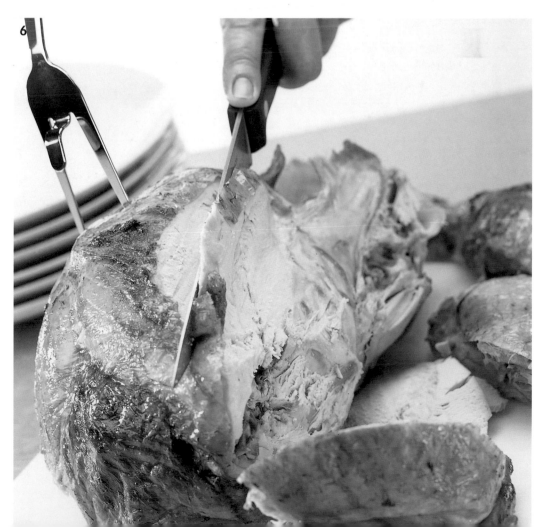

Roast Turkey with Chestnut and Apple Stuffing

The tartness of the apple counterbalances the richness of the meat in this classic festive dish.

Serves: **8**

Preparation time: about 30 minutes

Cooking time: 2¾–3¼ hours

Oven temperature: 190°C/375°F/Gas Mark 5

4.5–5.4 kg/10–12 lb oven-ready turkey
Chestnut and Apple Stuffing
1 small onion, peeled and halved
40 g/1½ oz butter, softened
2 tablespoons vegetable oil
salt and pepper
freshly cooked vegetables, to serve
TO GARNISH
fried apple rings
watercress sprigs

1 Wash the inside of the turkey and dry thoroughly with kitchen paper. Pack the stuffing loosely into the neck cavity of the bird. Smooth the skin back over and tuck underneath the bird to hold in place. Place the onion in the body cavity and season to taste with salt and pepper. Weigh the stuffed turkey and calculate the roasting time (see page 112)

2 Place the turkey in a large roasting tin and rub all over with butter. Add the oil to the tin and season the outside of the turkey with salt and pepper.

3 Roast in a preheated oven, 190°C/375°F/Gas mark 5, basting from time to time, for 2¾–3¼ hours, or until the juices run clear (see page 112). Cover with greaseproof paper or foil when the bird is sufficiently browned.

4 Transfer the turkey to a large dish. Pour off the fat from the tin and use the juices to make the gravy (see page 31).

5 Arrange the turkey on a warmed serving platter and serve with the gravy and an assortment of vegetables.

CHESTNUT AND APPLE STUFFING
Serves: **8**

Preparation time: 10 minutes

Cooking time: 10 minutes

500 g/1 lb chestnuts
4 shallots, finely chopped
1 tablespoon chopped parsley
1 small egg, beaten
500 g/1 lb dessert apples, peeled, cored and chopped
250 g/8 oz belly pork, finely chopped
salt and pepper

1 Cook the chestnuts in boiling water for 15 minutes. Drain, cool, peel and chop. Mix with the shallots, parsley, and egg and season with salt and pepper to taste.

2 Place the apples in a pan and cook, stirring, for 5 minutes. Mix into the stuffing, together with the pork.

FOOD TIP • Trussing the turkey will keep the stuffing in position and also hold the bird together, so that it will cook evenly and sit easily for carving. To do this, set it breast up and pull back the legs. Push a threaded trussing needle through the bird at the joint of the knee. Turn the bird on to its breast, pull the neck skin over the neck cavity and secure with a stitch, which passes through both the wings. Next, turn the bird on to its side, pull the ends of the string from both the leg and wing together and fasten them firmly. Finally, turn the bird breast side up, tuck the tail into the body cavity and tie the drumsticks together by stitching in a figure-of-eight under the breast bone and around the two drumsticks.

Duck Breasts with Balsamic Vinegar

In this dish, the cranberries break down and make a delicious sauce with the vinegar and duck juices. The duck breasts should be pink and juicy in the middle.

Serves: **4**

Preparation time: 5 minutes

Cooking time: 25 minutes

1 tablespoon vegetable oil
4 boneless duck breasts
4 tablespoons balsamic vinegar
75 g/3 oz frozen cranberries, defrosted
50 g/2 oz brown sugar
salt and pepper
freshly cooked vegetables, such as potatoes
 and asparagus, to serve

1 Heat the oil in a heavy-based frying pan. Add the duck breasts, skin side down, and cook over a moderate heat for 5 minutes, then reduce the heat and cook for a further 10 minutes. Drain the excess oil from the duck skin.

2 Turn the duck breasts over and add the balsamic vinegar, together with the cranberries and sugar. Season to taste with salt and pepper and cook for a further 10 minutes.

3 Serve the duck breast with the sauce spooned over, accompanied by freshly cooked vegetables.

FOOD FACT • Balsamic vinegar, which comes from the area around Modena in northern Italy, has a uniquely smooth sweet-and-sour flavour. It is made from grape juice concentrated over a low heat and then fermented in wooden barrels over several years. It is expensive, but a little goes a long way. It can also be used in salad dressings and a few drops will enrich meaty casseroles.

Pot Roast Chicken with Lemon and Rosemary

Serves: **4**

Preparation time: 5 minutes

Cooking time: about 1 hour 10 minutes

2 tablespoons olive oil

15 g/½ oz unsalted butter

1 chicken weighing about 1.75 kg/3½ lb, jointed

2 garlic cloves, finely crushed

125 ml/4 fl oz medium-bodied dry white wine

1 rosemary sprig

2 tablespoons lemon juice

5–6 fine strips of lemon rind

salt and pepper

TO SERVE

steamed Carrot and Courgette Ribbons (see page 142)

cooked long-grain rice (see page 67), mixed with chopped herbs

1 Heat the oil and butter in a heavy, flameproof casserole. Add the chicken, skin side down, and fry over a medium heat until lightly browned all over, adding the garlic towards the end.

2 Stir in the wine, add the rosemary and season to taste with salt and pepper. Bring to the boil for 2–3 minutes, then lower the heat, cover tightly and cook over a very low heat, turning the chicken a couple of times, for about 45-50 minutes, or until the juices run clear (see page 112).

3 Remove the chicken and transfer it to a warmed serving plate. Cover it and keep it warm in the oven with the heat turned off.

4 Meanwhile, make the sauce. Discard the rosemary and skim off most of the fat from the cooking juices. Stir in the lemon juice to dislodge the sediment. Add the strips of lemon rind and bring to the boil over a high heat, stirring constantly. Pour the sauce over the chicken and serve immediately with carrot and courgette ribbons and rice mixed with chopped herbs.

Tandoori Chicken

A tandoor is a very hot clay oven, but tandoori has now come to mean the spicy yogurt marinade that flavours the meat. Chicken is especially delicious cooked this way, but you could use lamb instead.

Serves: **4**

Preparation time: 10 minutes, plus marinating

Cooking time: 20 minutes

4 boneless, skinless chicken breasts
flat-leafed parsley sprigs, to garnish
TO SERVE
lime wedges
mixed salad (optional)

TANDOORI MARINADE
300 ml/½ pint natural yogurt
1 cm/½ inch piece fresh ginger root, finely chopped
1 garlic clove, minced
2 teaspoons paprika
1 teaspoon chilli powder
1 tablespoon tomato purée
finely grated rind and juice of ½ lemon
salt and pepper

1 Mix all the marinade ingredients together and season to taste with salt and pepper. Pour into a shallow, non-metallic dish. Prick the chicken breasts all over with a fine skewer and place in the marinade, turning to coat well. Cover and set aside to marinate overnight in a cool place, turning the chicken occasionally.

2 Remove the chicken from the marinade and place on an oiled preheated barbecue or the rack of a grill pan. Cook for about 10 minutes on each side, or until the chicken is tender and the juices run clear (see page 112).

3 Garnish with parsley sprigs and serve with lime wedges and a mixed salad, if liked.

FOOD FACT • Chilli powder may vary considerably from brand to brand. Some are made purely from dried chillies, while others may include additional spices.

Beef, Lamb and Pork

A Brief Guide to Meat Cuts

Beef

Brisket
Available as a boned and rolled joint, this cut is best braised or pot-roasted. It is a traditional cut for salting.

Chuck and Blade
Fairly lean cuts, with a slight marbling of fat, usually sold diced for stewing or braising.

Entrecôte
A slice cut from the sirloin or rump for grilling or frying.

Fillet
Lean and tender, this is a prime steak for grilling and frying.

Fore-rib, Wing Rib and Prime Rib
These roasting cuts have a good proportion of fat, giving them lots of flavour.

Neck or Clod
Economical cuts, usually sold diced for stewing or minced.

Rump
A fairly lean, tender cut, sold either as a rolled joint or in slices as steak for frying, grilling or braising.

Shin (foreleg) and Leg (hindleg)
These cuts contain a high proportion of connective tissue, so they need long stewing to tenderise.

Silverside
Tender and lean, this is best for pot-roasting since it can be dry if roasted.

Sirloin
A tender and lean, boned and rolled cut for roasting. Porterhouse steak and minute steak are both cut from sirloin.

Thick flank or Top Rump, Thin Flank
A lean joint, good for pot roasting or braising, or slices can be braised. Thin flank is often sold as mince.

Topside
A lean cut with little fat, traditionally sold rolled for roasting, with a layer of fat tied around it.

Lamb

Best End of Neck or Rack of Lamb
This is sold as a rack of 6–8 ribs, with the chine bone (running across them) removed for easy carving. Suitable for roasting, it is traditionally used for guard of honour and crown roast. It can also be separated into individual ribs to make cutlets.

Breast
A long, thin cut streaked with fat. It is usually boned and rolled, and often stuffed for slow roasting or braising.

Leg
A favourite roasting cut with a high proportion of lean meat, it is sold on the bone, whole or halved as shank or fillet end, or boned and rolled. It is also available sliced as leg steaks.

Loin and Saddle (Double Loin)
Loin, a roasting cut, is often divided into loin and chump end, or it can be sliced into chops. Saddle is a special-occasion roast; alternatively, it can be sliced into butterfly or Barnsley chops (double chops).

Scrag and Middle Neck
These are usually sold in the form of chops for stewing or braising.

Shoulder
A tender, succulent roasting joint, sold whole or halved, or sliced into chops or steaks.

Pork

Unlike beef and lamb, all pork meat is tender and suitable for roasting as well as braising or stewing. The difference between the cuts is in the amount of fat and sinews they contain. Slow roasting or pot-roasting is best for cuts with a higher proportion of fat.

Belly
A long cut, streaked with fat and lean, sold as slices, or as mince, or sometimes as a boned and rolled joint.

Leg
This is usually divided into knuckle and fillet end joints for roasting. The fillet end is also sliced into steaks.

Loin
A prime roasting cut sold on the bone or boned and rolled. It is also cut into steaks or chops (with or without kidney).

Chump End
This is usually sold as chops on the bone.

Hand and Spring (shoulder)
A large joint for roasting, often divided into hand and shank joints. It is also sold trimmed and diced for casseroling.

Neck End or Spare Rib and Blade Bone
Large joints, marbled with fat, often boned and rolled or divided into spare rib chops.

Tenderloin
A very tender, lean and versatile cut weighing about 375 g/12 oz.

Bacon and Ham
Cured pork, including bacon rashers and chops, joints of bacon or ham and gammon steaks. Lean cuts are tender for grilling and frying; joints can be boiled, braised or baked.

How Much Meat Should I Buy?

The amount of meat to buy very much depends on individual tastes and appetite, the type of meat and the way you plan to cook it. As a rough guide, allow 125–175 g/4–6 oz meat off the bone or 175–375 g/6–12 oz on the bone per portion. If the meat is cooked and served plain, choose the higher quantity.

Cuts for Roasting

Beef   sirloin, topside, boned and rolled prime rib, wing rib, fore-rib, rump or fillet

Lamb   leg, shoulder, loin, saddle, best end of neck, crown roast or guard of honour

Pork   loin, leg, hand or shoulder

Cuts for Stews, Casseroles or Braises

Beef   shin or leg, clod, chuck, blade, flank or skirt; pot-roasting: silverside or brisket

Lamb   leg, shoulder, loin chops, boned and rolled breast, neck and shank

Pork   blade, shoulder, leg steaks, loin, chump or spare rib chops; pot-roasting: leg, shoulder, belly, spare rib joint or hand and spring

Cuts for Frying, Grilling or Barbecues

Beef   sirloin, rump, fillet, entrecôte or porterhouse steaks

Lamb   neck fillet slices, loin, butterfly and chump chops, leg or chump steaks or cutlets

Pork   tenderloin, chump, spare rib or loin chops, loin or leg steaks, escalopes or belly slices.

How to Prepare Meat

Cutting Meat

When cutting meat into slices, steaks or strips, cut across the grain, since this will give tender results and the pieces will keep their shape better during cooking. Always cut dice or strips of meat to the same size, so that they cook evenly in the same time. To slice meat very thinly for stir-fries, freeze the meat for about 30 minutes in order to make it firm and easier to slice thinly.

Preparing Steaks or Chops

Before cooking a steak or chop with a rim of fat around the edge, snip into the fat at regular intervals to prevent it from curling up as it shrinks during cooking.

Tenderising Steak

Method 1

Place the steak between sheets of clingfilm or greaseproof paper and beat it with a meat hammer or a wooden rolling pin. This helps to break down the connective tissue that makes meat tough.

Method 2

Purée the flesh of a fresh papaya or kiwifruit and spread this over the surface of the meat. Cover and chill for 2–3 hours before cooking.

Method 3

Place the meat in a shallow dish and pour over just enough fresh pineapple juice to cover it. To tenderise liver, soak it in tomato juice. Cover and chill for 2–3 hours.

Mincing Meat in a Food Processor

Use the chopping blade attachment and pulse the power as you drop diced lean meat on to the blades of the food processor. Pulse the power until the meat is finely chopped. Take care not to overprocess the meat or it will become very soft and paste-like, losing its texture. For small meatballs the meat can be processed more finely; for example, kofta have a very smooth texture.

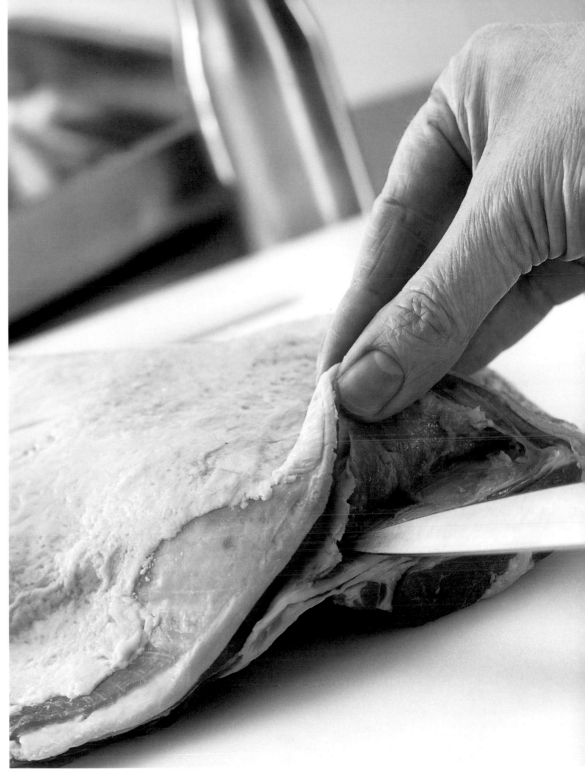

Stretching Bacon Rashers

Before rolling up streaky bacon, or when you are using it to line containers or to wrap food, it is advisable to stretch the rashers. Cut off the rind from each rasher. Place a rasher on a board and, using the flat blade of a knife, press firmly along the length of the rasher, stretching it as you go.

Preparing a Shoulder of Lamb for Roasting

Shoulder of lamb can be tricky to carve, but if you loosen the bladebone before cooking, the task becomes far easier. Feel along the cut edge of the shoulder to find the edge of the bladebone, then use a small sharp knife to separate it from the flesh on either side.

Continue cutting into the joint, as close to the bone as possible, and make sure the bladebone is loosened right down to the joint on both sides. After roasting the meat, grasp the blade-bone firmly with a cloth and twist it to break it free at the joint. You can then simply lift out the bone and the meat can be carved straight across the shoulder.

How to Cook Meat

The Perfect Steak

Steak may be grilled or fried: grilling is the healthier option since it is not necessary to add extra fat. Remember that leaner cuts may need less cooking time. Whichever method you choose, be sure to preheat the grill or frying pan to very hot before adding the meat, to seal in the juices and flavour. Once sealed, the heat may be reduced slightly.

	Rare	Medium	Well Done
Sirloin or rump, 1.5 cm/ ¾ inch thick	2½ mins	4 mins	6 mins
Fillet, 1.5–3 cm/ ¾–1½ inch thick	3–4 mins	4–5 mins	6–7 mins

Stewing and Braising Basics

1 Choose a heavy, flameproof casserole or a large pan with a tight-fitting lid. The pan can be covered closely, if necessary, by placing a double layer of foil over the top, under the lid.
2 It is important to brown the meat before adding liquid. This improves the flavour and colour, and helps to seal the juices into the meat. The oil or fat in the pan should be really hot before adding the meat. Brown the meat in small batches, removing it with a slotted spoon before adding another batch.
3 The liquid used depends on your recipe – well-flavoured stock, beer, cider or wine are ideal. Canned tomatoes or passata can also be used for flavour and moisture.
4 Once the stew is simmering, reduce the heat to very low – the slightest bubble is all that is needed. This will slowly tenderise ingredients and bring out their flavour. Boiling meat fiercely toughens it and makes it shrink.
5 The flavour of most stews and casseroles matures and improves if they are made a day in advance of being served. Cool the cooked casserole as quickly as possible, then place in the refrigerator and reheat thoroughly before serving.

Rules for Roasting Meat

1 Preheat the oven to the correct temperature – this way the surface of the meat begins to seal immediately it goes into the hot oven and it retains both juices and flavour.
2 Place the joint of meat, uncovered, on a rack in a roasting tin with the largest cut surfaces exposed to the heat. Any fat surface should be on the top, so that the joint is naturally basted as the fat melts during cooking. Baste the meat 2–3 times during roasting by spooning the cooking juices over it.
3 To test if meat is cooked, insert a skewer into the thickest part, near the bone if there is one, and look at the juices. For pork and veal, the juices should run clear in colour, with no trace of pink. Beef and lamb juices may be slightly pink if you like your meat medium, or clear and golden if you prefer it well-done.

4 Allow the cooked joint to stand in a warm place for 10–15 minutes to rest. This makes carving easier and the meat will be both better flavoured and tender.

Perfect Pork Crackling

1 For really good crackling, choose a joint that has thick, dry skin and a layer of fat. Dry the skin thoroughly with kitchen paper.
2 If your butcher has not already scored the rind of the pork, do this with a very sharp, rigid knife. The cuts should go all around the skin and they should be deep enough to penetrate the fat without going right through to the flesh.
3 Rub the surface of the skin with a little sunflower oil, then sprinkle it generously with salt. Roast the joint with the skin uppermost and do not baste during cooking.

Simple Flavourings for Plain Roasts

Mustard
Rub mustard powder into the surface of fatty cuts of beef or pork before roasting.

Garlic and Rosemary
Stud a lamb or beef joint with garlic before roasting. Make deep, but narrow, cuts all over the joint with the tip of a knife and slip slivers of peeled garlic cloves and rosemary leaves into the slits.

Horseradish
Mix equal quantities of creamed horseradish and dry white breadcrumbs. Spread the mixture over the surface of a beef joint for the final 20 minutes of roasting.

Pesto
Mix a little pesto (see page 37) with fresh breadcrumbs, then spread over the surface of a roast for the final 20 minutes of roasting.

Using a Meat Thermometer

To take the guesswork out of checking whether meat is cooked, insert a meat thermometer into the thickest part of the joint but not touching the bone or fat. Check the temperature: for rare meat it should be 60°C/140°F; for medium it should read 70–75°C/158–167°F; and for well-done meat the temperature should be 80–85°C/176–185°F.

Roasting Times for Meat
(at cooking temperature 180°C/350°F/Mark 4

	Rare	Medium	Well Done
Beef	20 mins per 500 g/1 lb plus 20 mins	25 mins per 500 g/1 lb plus 25 mins	30 mins per 500 g/1 lb plus 30 mins
Lamb		25 mins per 500 g/1 lb plus 25 mins	30 mins per 500 g/1 lb plus 30 mins
Pork		30 mins per 500 g/1 lb plus 30 mins	35 mins per 500 g/1 lb plus 35 mins

Lamb and Courgette Koftas

These delicious little meatballs are both quick and easy to make and may be served as part of a main meal with rice or as a speedy lunchtime snack.

Serves: **4**

Preparation time: 20 minutes

Cooking time: 5 minutes each batch

2 courgettes, finely grated
2 tablespoons sesame seeds
250 g/8 oz minced lamb
2 spring onions, finely chopped
1 garlic clove, crushed
1 tablespoon chopped mint
½ teaspoon ground mixed spice
2 tablespoons dried breadcrumbs
1 egg, lightly beaten
vegetable oil, for shallow-frying
salt and pepper
lemon wedges, to garnish

1 Place the finely grated courgettes in a sieve and press down to extract as much liquid as possible. Place in a bowl.

2 Dry-fry the sesame seeds in a heavy-based frying pan for 1–2 minutes, until they are golden and release their aroma. Add to the courgettes, together with the lamb and all the remaining ingredients, except the oil and lemon. Season liberally with salt and pepper.

3 Form the mixture into 20 small balls and shallow-fry in batches for 5 minutes, turning frequently until evenly browned. Keep the koftas warm in a hot oven while you are cooking the rest. Serve hot, garnished with lemon wedges.

FOOD FACT • Even if you buy ready-minced lamb, it is worth working it in a food processor (see page 127) or mincer before making the koftas to ensure that it is really finely minced. If you buy the lamb in one piece, process it twice in the food processor or mincer before adding it to the other ingredients.

Tangerine Beef

This easy-to-make stir-fry uses tangerine segments for additional flavour and colour – a perfect dish for winter when tangerines are in season. It is a classic dish from Canton in southern China.

Serves: **2–3**

Preparation time: about 15 minutes, plus freezing and marinating

Cooking time: 15 minutes

1 piece of rump steak, weighing about 375 g/12 oz
3 tablespoons groundnut oil
4 shallots, cut lengthways into chunks
200 ml/7 fl oz Beef Stock (see page 38) or water
2 tablespoons soy sauce
2 tablespoons Chinese rice wine or dry sherry
3 tangerines, peeled and segmented, with their juice
1 green chilli, deseeded and very finely chopped
1–2 teaspoons sugar
salt and pepper
½ bunch coriander, roughly chopped, to garnish
MARINADE
2 pieces of dried citrus fruit peel or grated rind of 1 orange
2 tablespoons soy sauce
1 tablespoon rice wine vinegar or white wine or cider vinegar
1 tablespoon cornflour
1 teaspoon sugar

1 Wrap the beef in clingfilm and place it in the freezer for 1–2 hours until it has become quite firm. Meanwhile, if using, soak the pieces of citrus peel for the marinade in hot water for about 30 minutes until softened, then drain and chop finely.

2 Remove the beef from the freezer, unwrap it and slice it into thin strips against the grain. Put the strips in a non-metallic dish. Whisk together all the marinade ingredients, including the grated orange rind, if using, pour the marinade over the beef and stir to coat thoroughly. Set aside to marinate at room temperature for about 30 minutes, or until the beef is completely thawed.

3 Preheat a wok or large, heavy-based frying pan. Add 1 tablespoon of the oil, swirl it around the pan and heat until hot. Add about half the beef and stir-fry over a high heat for 3 minutes. Transfer the beef to a plate using a slotted spoon. Add 1 further tablespoon of oil to the pan and stir-fry the remaining beef in the same way. Transfer to the plate using a slotted spoon.

4 Heat the remaining oil in the wok or pan, then add the shallots, stock or water, soy sauce, Chinese rice wine or sherry and the juice from the tangerines. Sprinkle in the chilli, sugar to taste and a little salt and pepper. Bring to the boil, stirring constantly, then stir-fry for about 5 minutes, until the liquid has reduced.

5 Return the beef to the pan and toss vigorously for 1–2 minutes until all the ingredients are combined and coated with sauce. Add about two-thirds of the tangerine segments and toss quickly to mix, then taste for seasoning and adjust if necesssary. Serve hot, strewn with the remaining tangerine segments and the coriander.

FOOD FACT • Dried citrus fruit peel, including tangerine peel, is sold in packets in Chinese foodstores and some supermarkets. For advice on segmenting citrus fruit, see page 166.

Lamb Chops in Red Wine and Mint

Serves: **4**

Preparation time: 5 minutes, plus marinating

Cooking time: 15–20 minutes

8 lamb chops or lamb leg steaks, about 2.5 cm/
  1 inch thick
175 ml/6 fl oz red wine
4½ teaspoons olive oil
5 tablespoons finely chopped mint
salt and pepper
mixed leaf salad, to serve (optional)
YOGURT DIP
2 tablespoons olive oil
4½ teaspoons lime juice
1 small onion, shredded
1 teaspoon ground cloves
1 teaspoon cumin seeds, crushed
¼ teaspoon ground cardamom
2 garlic cloves, minced
1 teaspoon ground cinnamon
1 teaspoon salt
1 teaspoon freshly ground white pepper
TO GARNISH
mint or parsley sprigs
tomato wedges

1 Put the lamb chops or steaks in a shallow, non-metallic dish. Mix together the wine, oil and chopped mint, then pour the mixture over the meat, turning to coat thoroughly. Cover and set aside to marinate in a cool place for 1 hour, turning halfway through.

2 Remove the lamb from the marinade and cook on a preheated greased barbecue grill or under a conventional grill for 7–10 minutes on each side, depending on whether you like your lamb rare or well done. Baste with any leftover marinade before turning.

3 Meanwhile, make the yogurt dip by mixing all the ingredients together in a small serving bowl. Chill in the refrigerator until required.

4 Sprinkle the lamb with salt and pepper to taste and serve very hot, garnished with the mint or parsley and tomato wedges and accompanied by the yogurt dip. Serve with a mixed salad, if liked.

Roast Pork with Bulgar and Celery Stuffing

Serves: **6**

Preparation time: 15 minutes

Cooking time: about 2½ hours

Oven temperature: 160°C/325°F/Gas Mark 3

1.75 kg/3½ lb pork loin joint
50 g/2 oz bulgar wheat
300 ml/½ pint boiling water
1 small onion, finely chopped
2 celery sticks, finely chopped
50 g/2 oz mushrooms, finely chopped
1 tablespoon chopped sage
2 tablespoons natural yogurt
salt and pepper

1 Remove the skin and most of the fat from the pork, leaving only a thin layer, then score the surface into a diamond pattern. Turn the meat over and, using a sharp knife, remove the bones.

2 Place the bulgar wheat in a saucepan, pour over the water and bring back to the boil. Cover and simmer for 10–15 minutes, or until the liquid is absorbed. Stir in the onion, celery, mushrooms, sage and yogurt and season to taste with salt and pepper.

3 Spread the stuffing over the pork, roll up and tie with fine cotton string. Place the pork on a rack in a roasting tin and sprinkle with pepper. Roast in a preheated oven, 160°C/325°F/Gas Mark 3, basting occasionally with the juices in the tin, for about 2 hours, until the juices run clear (see page 128). Garnish with celery leaves. Skim the juices and serve as a gravy (see page 31).

Vegetables and Salads

Buying Vegetables

Brassicas and Leaves

These include broccoli, sprouting broccoli, cauliflower, kale, sprouts, pak-choi, cabbages, spring greens, Chinese leaf, kohlrabi, spinach and lettuce (see also Types of Salad Leaves, pages 154–155). All brassicas and leaves should be eaten as fresh as possible, so look for crisp leaves or heads with a bright, fresh colour. Broccoli and cauliflower should have firm, tightly packed heads; avoid loose, 'blown' or damaged florets.

Loose leaves, such as spring greens, sweetheart cabbage, kale or spinach, wilt quickly, so use them as soon as possible. Other cabbages and Brussels sprouts should be firm and close-packed, with an overall fresh appearance and no sign of yellowing or bruising of the leaves.

Full-hearted, pointed green cabbages tend to have a sweeter flavour than many of the round varieties, so these are a good choice for a plainly cooked side dish.

Pods and Seeds

This group of vegetables includes sweetcorn, mangetout, peas, sugar snap peas, okra, broad beans and green beans, such as runner beans and French beans.

When choosing any pods, look for a bright and succulent appearance, and avoid any pods that are wet or grey in colour. Bean pods should break cleanly – a fresh French bean will snap between finger and thumb. Avoid any beans that look old, distorted or badly curled. Broad beans should have soft, tender pods with young, rather than fully mature, beans inside. Peas should be sweet and tender enough to be eaten raw; fresh peas will disintegrate under gentle pressure between finger and thumb. Sweetcorn tastes best only minutes after it is picked, so the fresher the better. Choose young and tender cobs with fresh-looking, slightly green husks. The cob should be full and plump, with bright, shiny and juicy grains.

Shoots

These include celery, asparagus, globe artichokes, fennel, bamboo shoots and chicory. All fresh shoots should look firm and crisp – any with limp or dried-out parts should be avoided. Asparagus quickly loses flavour in storage, so eat it on the day of purchase if possible. The buds should be tight and the spears fresh and bright in colour. Early, thin asparagus, called sprue, is very tender and it needs only the minimum of cooking.

Very young, tender globe artichokes can be trimmed and added to casseroles, but larger, mature vegetables have to be trimmed. Use scissors to snip off the leaf ends, remove the middle of each vegetable and scoop out the hairy choke. Choose plump, fresh-looking globes without brown patches or dried parts.

Both white and green celery and fennel should look firm and clean. Damaged or bruised vegetables will deteriorate quickly. The top leaves are usually trimmed off, since this helps to keep the stems fresh for longer.

Bulbs

These include all types of onions – Spanish, red, white, yellow, spring onions, shallots, pickling onions and leeks. All bulbs should look bright and crisp when you buy them. Avoid any that are sprouting, damp or soft. The many varieties of onions vary widely in colour, but in all cases the skins should be dry, light and feathery. Onions keep well in a cool, dry place, but use them up quickly if they show signs of damage or sprouting.

Leeks and spring onions should have bright green tops. Generally, the thinner they are, the milder their flavour and more delicate their texture. These vegetables are best used within 1–2 days, but they can be stored in the refrigerator, if necessary.

Roots and Tubers

Roots include beetroot, carrots, celeriac, parsnips, swedes, turnips, radish, salsify, etc. Tubers include all types of potato, yams, sweet potato and Jerusalem artichokes.

Fungi

These include all types of mushrooms, such as button, open-cup, flat, oyster, shiitake, ceps, chanterelles, morels, truffles and straw mushrooms. Ordinary cultivated mushrooms, whether button, closed-cup, open-cup or flat, should be clean and white. Chestnut mushrooms have a delicate brown colour, a firm cap and fleshy stem. Shiitake and oyster mushrooms are cultivated.

All these vegetables should be firm and dry, with no sign of wrinkling or damage. Avoid potatoes that are sprouting or with green patches. Most early potatoes are good for salads and boiling. Jersey Royals have an excellent flavour, but buy them when they are very fresh – the skins should rub off easily with a fingertip. Later season, larger potatoes are best for chipping and baking.

To test an avocado for ripeness, cup it gently in your hand and apply gentle pressure to feel it without actually squeezing – the avocado should yield slightly without feeling squashy.

All mushrooms should be bought in small quantities and often, as they are best eaten within 3 days of purchase. Never wash them before storage, but simply place in a paper bag inside a polythene bag and keep in the bottom of the refrigerator.

Fruit Vegetables

These include peppers, chillies, aubergines, tomatoes and avocados. Peppers, aubergines, tomatoes and chillies should all have brightly coloured, shiny skins. They should be firm, without discoloured, wrinkled or soft patches. A green, fresh-looking calyx (the leafy part at the stem end) is a good indication of freshness. Store in a cool place, but not too cold – tomatoes in particular can become hard and tasteless if stored at low temperatures for long periods.

Squashes and Cucumbers

These include all types of squash (such as acorn, butternut, spaghetti and patty pan), pumpkins, marrows, courgettes and cucumbers. These versatile vegetables keep very well as long as they are undamaged, so inspect them closely, particularly for soft parts.

Tender-skinned, summer squashes should be firm, shiny and smooth, and your fingernail should be able to pierce the skin. Hard-skinned winter squashes have a very firm skin that helps to keep them fresh for months. Courgettes should be small, plump and glossy; larger ones are useful for stuffing. Marrows should not be overlarge since they become tough and tasteless with age.

How to Prepare Vegetables

Slicing Onions

Using a sharp knife, cut the onion in half, cutting through the root. Peel both halves, but leave the root intact, since this helps to reduce the eye-stinging effect of onion, and also gives you something to hold when cutting. Place one onion half cut-side down on a board and, using your knuckles as a guide, slice down with a forward action.

Chopping Onions

Peel and halve the onion as above, then place one half cut-side down on a board. Cut horizontal slices in towards the root but not right through it. Holding the root end, make vertical cuts from the root end, keeping all the pieces in place. Finally, slice across and the onion will fall apart into small pieces.

Peeling Tomatoes

Method 1

Drop whole tomatoes into a saucepan of boiling water and leave for 1 minute. Lift out with a slotted spoon and drop into a bowl of cold water. The skins will peel off easily once slit.

Method 2

If you have a gas hob, spear a tomato firmly on a fork, then hold it in the flame. Turn the tomato evenly until the skin blisters and splits, when it will peel off easily.

Preparing Chillies

When preparing chillies, it is a good idea to wear rubber gloves since the juices from the seeds and flesh can irritate the eyes and skin. Alternatively, wash your hands thoroughly after preparing the chillies and avoid touching your eyes until your hands are thoroughly clean.

The seeds are the hottest part of the chilli, so for a slightly milder flavour, you may prefer to remove the seeds before use. Discard the stalk from the chilli and cut it in half lengthways. Use the tip of a sharp knife to scrape out the seeds and pith from the centre. Slice or chop the flesh of the chilli.

Cutting Julienne Strips

Trim the vegetables or peel thinly, then cut them into 6 cm/2½ inch lengths. Slice the lengths into 3 mm/⅛ inch thick slices. Stack the slices, hold them together firmly, then slice them lengthways, as thinly as possible, to make thin matchstick strips.

Making Vegetable Ribbons

This works well with carrots and courgettes. The ribbons can be stir-fried, steamed or served raw in salads. Prepare the courgettes or carrots, leaving their tops in place. Holding the top firmly, use a vegetable peeler to pare fine ribbons down the length of the vegetable, then discard the top.

Shredding Cabbage

Separate the leaves and cut away any thick stalk ends. Roll up several leaves together firmly. Holding the rolled leaves securely together, use a sharp knife to slice across the roll – the cabbage will fall away in fine shreds.

Peeling Peppers

The easiest way to remove the skins from peppers is to grill them until blistered and charred. This also tenderises the flesh and improves its flavour. Preheat the grill on the hottest setting. Cut the peppers in half and remove the seeds and core. Place cut side down on a foil-lined grill pan, and place under the hot grill. Grill until the skins are blackened and split. Alternatively, grill the peppers skin side down over a moderately hot barbecue. Remove from the heat and cover the peppers loosely with foil or a cloth, then leave until cool enough to handle, when the skins will peel off easily.

Salting Aubergines

To remove the bitter juices from aubergines, and to help them absorb less oil during cooking, salt them before use. Slice or dice the aubergine, depending on your recipe, then place it in a colander, sprinkling liberally with salt between layers. Leave to drain for about 30 minutes, then rinse under cold running water and dry on kitchen paper. If you plan to cook the aubergines in halves, score the cut surface of the flesh deeply in a diamond pattern with a sharp knife and sprinkle with salt, then drain and rinse.

To Crush Garlic

To crush garlic without a garlic crusher, place the unpeeled clove on a board. Hit the garlic sharply with the flat blade of a heavy knife. Peel off the skin, then sprinkle with a little salt and chop. Press with the flat of the knife to mash the garlic to a paste.

Preparing Asparagus

Very thin, sprue asparagus does not have to be peeled, but larger spears usually require some trimming. Slice or break off the woody ends of larger spears. Use a vegetable peeler to shave off any tough outer skin at the base. Trim the stalks to the same length for cooking.

Trimming Sprouts

To prepare sprouts for cooking, trim a thin slice from the stalk end and remove any loose or damaged outer leaves. Cut a cross into the base of the core so that it cooks as quickly as the outer leaves. For stir-fries or to be eaten raw in salads, shred the sprouts finely.

How to Cook Vegetables

Roasting Garlic

Roasting transforms pungent garlic, giving it a subtle, caramel-like flavour. Add the tender pulp from the roasted cloves to soups, stews or salsas; smear it over grilled meats; tuck it into baked jacket potatoes; or simply spread it on to grilled slices of ciabatta bread to make a savoury snack or accompaniment for main dishes. Place the whole garlic head on a square of foil on a baking sheet and drizzle with olive oil. Wrap the foil around the garlic to enclose it completely and roast in a preheated oven at 200°C/400°F/Gas Mark 6 for 20–25 minutes, turning occasionally, until soft and lightly browned. Snip the top from each clove and squeeze out the pulp.

Cooking Asparagus

Method 1

Arrange the asparagus in a single layer on a baking sheet or in an ovenproof dish. Drizzle with olive oil and lemon juice, and sprinkle with salt and pepper. Cover with foil and cook in a preheated oven at 190°C/375°F/Gas Mark 5 for 20–25 minutes or until tender. The cooking time will vary depending on the age and thickness of the spears.

Method 2

Tie the trimmed asparagus stems together in bundles. Wedge the bundles upright in a large, deep saucepan of boiling water: the water should come about half-way up the spears. If possible, cover with a lid, or if the tips stand above the top of the pan, make a foil cover. Simmer for 8–12 minutes, depending on thickness and age, until tender. The tips will cook gently in the steam, so they will not overcook.

Roasting Vegetables

Most vegetables respond well to this method and it is a very easy way to cook a variety of vegetables together, especially if you are

roasting a joint of meat or baking a main dish at the same time. Choose a selection of root vegetables, such as carrots, turnips, parsnips, swede and beetroot, or a Mediterranean style mixture of vegetables, such as aubergine, courgettes, peppers, fennel, red onions and plum tomatoes.

Prepare the vegetables according to type and cut them into large, even-sized pieces or keep baby vegetables whole. Arrange them in a single layer in a large roasting tin and drizzle with olive oil. Tuck cloves of garlic and sprigs of thyme or rosemary between the vegetables, then sprinkle with salt and pepper. Roast in a preheated oven at 220°C/425°F/Gas Mark 7 for 30–40 minutes or until tender and golden, turning occasionally.

The Perfect Mash

This method and its variations are suitable for potatoes or other roots, such as parsnips, turnips, sweet potato and swede. For potato mash, choose a floury variety of potato, such as Pentland Squire, Romano or King Edward.

Basic Mash Recipe

Serves: **4**
Preparation time: about 10 minutes
Cooking time: about 20 minutes

750 g/1½ lb potatoes or other root vegetables
salt and pepper
100 ml/3½ fl oz milk
25 g/1 oz butter or 2 tablespoons olive oil

1 Cut the potatoes into even-sized chunks

and add them to a saucepan of boiling, lightly salted water. Cover and simmer for 20 minutes or until tender. Drain the potatoes and return them to the pan.

2 Meanwhile, heat the milk until almost boiling, then pour it over the potatoes. Add the butter or oil and mash the potatoes until smooth. Do not use a food processor, since this is too harsh and willl make the potatoes glue-like in texture.

3 Adjust the seasoning to taste and serve immediately. If the mash must be kept hot, cover the pan with a clean tea towel instead of a lid, to keep it fluffy.

Flavoured Mash

Apple and Bacon Mash

Peel, core and roughly chop 1 Bramley cooking apple and cook it gently in 3 tablespoons water and 1 tablespoon lemon juice until soft. Mash with the potato, then stir in 25 g/1 oz finely diced, crisply fried bacon.

Garlic and Herb Mash

Add the pulp from 2–3 cloves of roasted garlic to the potato before mashing, then stir in a handful of finely chopped thyme, rosemary, parsley or basil.

Lemon-mustard Mash

Stir 1 tablespoon wholegrain mustard and the finely grated rind of 1 lemon into the mash.

Minted Mash

Stir 2 tablespoons chopped fresh mint and 2 tablespoons crème fraîche into the mash.

Making Perfect Roast Potatoes

For really crisp, golden roasties, choose the most suitable varieties – Nadine, Wilja, Desirée, Maris Piper, Romano or King Edward. This method can be used for parsnips.

1 Peel the potatoes and cut into even-sized chunks – ideally about 4 cm/1½ inches in diameter.

2 Par-boil the potatoes in lightly salted, boiling water for 5 minutes. Drain well, then return the potatoes to the pan and cover with a lid. Shake the pan to slightly roughen up the surface of the potatoes.

3 Pour 1 tablespoon oil for every 500 g/1 lb potatoes into a large roasting tin and place it in a preheated oven at 220°C/425°F/Gas Mark 7 for a few minutes or until very hot.

4 Tip the potatoes into the hot oil and turn them to coat them lightly all over with the oil. Roast the potatoes for 45–50 minutes, turning them twice during the process, until they are golden and crunchy.

5 Drain on kitchen paper before serving, lightly sprinkled with salt.

Microwave Potato Wedges

This is the quickest way to cook a single portion of potatoes. Any potato variety can be used.

1 Scrub a 250 g/8 oz potato and dry it well. Cut it in half lengthways, then cut each half lengthways into four wedges.

2 Arrange the potatoes in a single layer in a microwaveproof dish and cover loosely with microwave film.

3 Cook on high (100% power) for 5–6 minutes or until tender.

4 Serve plain, or sprinkle with grated Cheddar cheese and microwave for 1 minute more on high (100% power) or place under a hot grill until golden.

Stir-frying Spinach

If you do not like soggy spinach, try stir-frying it instead of the usual steaming. Wash and drain the spinach. Heat a little oil in a wok or large saucepan and add the spinach. Stir lightly over a high heat until wilted. The moisture in the spinach will evaporate and it will be perfectly cooked in a matter of minutes, with no liquid to drain off. A little grated nutmeg enhances the flavour of spinach.

Cooking Cabbage

If you find plain cooked cabbage dull, try these simple ways to add flavour and variety.

Braised Cabbage

Finely shred the cabbage and simmer it in a small amount of well-flavoured stock and a knob of butter. Cook, covered, for about 4–5 minutes, shaking the pan occasionally to prevent sticking. Sprinkle with pepper before serving. For a different flavour, add a few crushed juniper berries or coriander seeds.

Steamed Wedges

Trim a whole cabbage, then cut it into slim wedges leaving the core intact to keep the leaves in shape. Arrange the cabbage in a steamer and cook over boiling water for 6–8 minutes, or until just tender. Drizzle with walnut oil or olive oil and sprinkle with grated lemon rind before serving.

Stir-fried Greens

Heat a small amount of oil in a wok and add 1 teaspoon each of finely chopped fresh root ginger and garlic. Stir-fry for 30 seconds, then add finely shredded green cabbage and stir-fry for 4–5 minutes or until just tender. Sprinkle with sesame seeds and serve.

Vegetable Purées

Almost any vegetable can be served as a purée, but carrots, parsnips, broad beans, spinach, pumpkin, sweet potato or celeriac are particularly successful. This is also a good method for rescuing vegetables that have slightly overcooked.

1 Steam or boil the prepared vegetables until tender, then drain thoroughly. Alternatively, simmer the vegetables in a small amount of stock and reserve 2–3 tablespoons of the cooking liquid for adding to the purée.
2 Process the vegetables in a food processor, use a hand blender or press them through a fine sieve or mouli until just smooth. Do not overprocess the vegetables or their texture will be spoiled.
3 Stir in a little cream or butter and season to taste with salt and pepper.

Flavouring Purées

Carrots: Grated ginger, butter and chives
Spinach: Crème fraîche and nutmeg
Parsnips: Chopped fresh sage, with a little walnut or hazelnut oil
Pumpkin: Garlic and soured cream
Sweet Potato: Grated Parmesan and thyme
Celeriac: Apple purée and a pinch of cloves and chopped fresh parsley

Cooking and Serving Squashes

All varieties of squash can be eaten as a vegetable accompaniment to meats, or served as a vegetarian main course. The following are basic cooking methods for squash.

Baking

Halve the squash and discard the seeds, but leave the skin on. Brush the cut surface with oil and place cut side down on a baking sheet. Cover with foil and bake in a preheated oven at 190°C/375°F/Gas Mark 5 until the flesh is tender. The time varies according to the size and type of squash. For example, an average butternut will take 50–60 minutes to cook. When cooked, scoop out the flesh and dice or mash to serve. Spaghetti squash is best cooked in this way – its spaghetti-like strands can then be scooped out and tossed with butter and grated Parmesan cheese.

Roasting

Peel and deseed the squash, then cut it into 4 cm/1½ inch chunks. Par-boil in lightly salted

boiling water for 3–4 minutes, then drain well. Toss lightly in oil, season with salt and pepper and, if you like, add a few sprigs of fresh thyme or rosemary. Turn into a roasting tin and cook in a preheated oven at 220°C/425°F/Gas Mark 7 for 20–25 minutes, until the squash are tender and golden brown.

Braising

Peel and deseed the squash, then cut it into 2.5 cm/1 inch dice. Small squash, such as patty pans, can be halved or thickly slice courgettes. Heat 25 g/1 oz butter and 2–3 tablespoons stock per 500 g/1 lb squash in a saucepan. Add the squash, season well, cover and simmer, shaking the pan occasionally, for 10–12 minutes or until tender. To serve, sprinkle with lime juice and chopped fresh herbs, such as parsley and chives.

Potato, Mushroom and Bacon Gratin

Use a floury potato for this dish, such as Maris Piper, King Edward or Pentland Squire, which will absorb the cooking juices and make the sauce thick and rich.

Serves: **4**

Preparation time: 10 minutes

Cooking time: 40–45 minutes

Oven temperature: 180°C/350°F/Gas Mark 4

20 g/¾ oz butter
4½ teaspoons olive oil
8 slices of lean bacon, rinded and cut into strips
1 large onion, minced
2 garlic cloves, crushed
25 g/1 oz mushrooms, sliced
750 g–1 kg/1½–2 lb cooked potatoes (boiled or steamed with their skins on)
150–175 ml/5–6 fl oz double cream
1 tablespoon minced parsley
5 tablespoons grated Cheddar cheese
3 tablespoons freshly grated Parmesan cheese
salt and pepper

1 Melt half the butter together with half the oil in a frying pan. Add the bacon and fry until it is beginning to brown. Remove from the pan with a slotted spoon and place in a large bowl.

2 Add the remaining butter and oil and fry the onion and garlic over a medium heat, stirring occasionally, for 5 minutes, until soft. Add the mushrooms and continue to fry until all the vegetables are beginning to colour. Using a slotted spoon, transfer all the vegetables to the bowl with the bacon and mix together.

3 Cut the potatoes into wedges and arrange them with the other vegetables in an ovenproof gratin dish. Mix the cream with the parsley, season to taste with salt and pepper and pour it over the vegetables. Mix the Cheddar and Parmesan cheeses together and scatter on top. Stand the dish on a baking sheet and bake in a preheated oven, 180°C/350°F/Gas Mark 4, for 20–30 minutes until crisp and golden. Serve immediately.

Ratatouille

This vegetable stew is one of the great dishes of the Mediterranean. In this version, the vegetables are roasted in the oven before they are combined with stewed tomatoes and herbs, to add flavour, richness and texture to the mixture. Ratatouille can be served hot or cold with crusty bread; as an accompaniment to meats or poultry; as a pasta sauce or as a filling for omelettes, pastry tarts or other vegetables such as courgettes or aubergines.

Serves: **8–9**

Preparation time: 10 minutes

Cooking time: 30 minutes

Oven temperature: 220°C/425°F/Gas Mark 7

125 ml/4 fl oz olive oil
2 large aubergines, quartered lengthways and cut into 1 cm/½ inch slices
2 courgettes, cut into 1 cm/½ inch slices
2 large red peppers, deseeded and cut into squares
1 large yellow pepper, deseeded and cut into squares
2 large onions, thinly sliced
3 large garlic cloves, crushed
1 tablespoon double concentrate tomato purée
400 g/13 oz can plum tomatoes
12 basil leaves, chopped
1 tablespoon finely chopped marjoram or oregano
1 teaspoon finely chopped thyme
1 tablespoon paprika
2–4 tablespoons finely chopped parsley
salt and pepper

1 Heat half the oil in a roasting tin in a preheated oven, 220°C/425°F/Gas Mark 7. Add the aubergines, courgettes and peppers, toss in the hot oil, return to the oven and roast for about 30 minutes, until tender.

2 While the vegetables are roasting, heat the remaining oil in a deep saucepan. Add the onions and garlic and fry over a medium heat, stirring occasionally, for 3–5 minutes, until soft but not coloured. Add the tomato purée, plum tomatoes, basil, marjoram or oregano, thyme and paprika and season to taste with salt and pepper. Stir to combine, then cook for 10–15 minutes until the mixture is thick and syrupy.

3 Using a slotted spoon, transfer the vegetables from the roasting tin to the tomato mixture. Gently stir to combine, then add the parsley and taste for seasoning. Serve the dish hot or cold.

Mixed Vegetable Curry

Serves: **4 as a main dish or 6 as a side dish**

Preparation time: 15 minutes

Cooking time: 20–25 minutes

2–3 tablespoons vegetable oil

1 small onion, chopped or 2 teaspoons cumin
 seeds

500 g/1 lb mixed vegetables, such as potatoes,
 carrots, swede, peas, French beans,
 cauliflower, cut into chunks or broken into
 florets (French beans can be left whole)

about 1 teaspoon chilli powder

2 teaspoons ground coriander

½ teaspoon ground turmeric

salt

2–3 tomatoes, skinned and chopped, or juice of
 1 lemon

300 ml/½ pint water (optional)

naan, chappatis or cooked Basmati rice
 (see page 64), to serve

1 Heat the oil in a heavy-based saucepan.
Add the onion and fry over a medium heat,
stirring occasionally, until light brown.
Alternatively, fry the cumin seeds until they
pop. Add the diced vegetables and stir in the
chilli powder, ground coriander, turmeric and
salt to taste. Fry for 2–3 minutes.

2 Add the chopped tomatoes or the lemon
juice. Stir well and add only a little water if a
dry vegetable curry is preferred. Cover and
cook gently for 10–12 minutes, until dry. For a
moister curry, stir in 300 ml/½ pint water
before covering and simmer for 5–6 minutes,
until the vegetables are tender.

3 Serve as a main dish with naan, chappatis
or rice, or on its own as a side dish.

Types of Salad Leaves

Iceberg Lettuce

This has the outside leaves removed, leaving just the crisp-textured, firm heart. To remove the core, leaving the leaves whole, slam the lettuce, stem end down, on to a worksurface, then pull out the core. Iceberg keeps for up to a week in the refrigerator. Iceberg lettuce is usually shredded, but the leaves can also be torn into pieces.

Cos and Little Gem Lettuce

This large lettuce has long, bright-green leaves with a good flavour and crisp texture. Little Gem lettuce, related to the Cos, is usually sold as small hearts and keeps well.

Butterhead Lettuce

A year-round lettuce with soft-textured leaves having a delicate, buttery flavour. This lettuce does not keep well. For best results, place the stem end in a bowl containing 1.5 cm/¾ inch cold water. Cover the bowl with clingfilm and place in the refrigerator for up to 2 days.

Oak Leaf Lettuce or *Feuille de Chêne*

This has long, scalloped leaves, tinged russet-red at the edges. It has a delicate flavour (which is very good with goat's cheese) and is useful for adding colour to mixed-leaf salads.

Lollo Rosso and Lollo Biondo

Lollo Rosso has attractive bright green, frilly leaves with red-fringed edges, and Lollo Biondo has frilly paler green leaves. Both have a good flavour and are excellent in salads or as a garnish, but they do not keep well.

Lamb's Lettuce

These small, long, smooth, green leaves have a sweet, fine flavour and tender texture. A few leaves can be mixed with other lettuce to good effect, or a cluster of leaves makes an elegant garnish.

Curly Endive or Frisée

This has very curly leaves, pale yellow in the centre and rich, bright green around the edges. The outer green leaves are more bitter than the pale central leaves. It is useful for mixing with other leaves and is good with warm dressings. It also makes a pretty garnish.

Batavia or Escarole

This is a broad-leafed member of the endive (or chicory) family, with a wide head of sturdy leaves and a pale yellow centre surrounded by darker green leaves. The leaves have a slightly bitter taste that complements strong flavours, such as goat's cheese, and warm salad dressings.

Radicchio

Also a member of the chicory family, its deep claret-red leaves add colour to leafy salads and garnishes. The crisp leaves have a bitter taste that goes well with fruity flavours and strongly flavoured dressings, such as those made with citrus juice or walnut oil.

Chicory or Whitloof

This has close-packed, spear-shaped leaves with a crisp texture and slightly bitter flavour. It is grown in the dark to keep the leaves white – too much green indicates that the leaves will taste bitter. Red-leafed chicory is also available and makes an unusual colour addition to salads.

Spinach

This is an all-year-round vegetable providing dark green leaves. Small summer leaves are tender and delicate in flavour, so they can be added whole to salads. Baby spinach, the tiny central leaves, are ideal for salads. Winter

spinach leaves are coarser in texture with a stronger flavour and are not as well suited to serving raw, but you can discard the stalks and shred the leaves for salads.

Chard
This is actually a variety of beetroot grown for its leaves. Swiss chard, or white beet, is usually cooked, but the white-stemmed leaves can be shredded to add raw to salads. Red chard has attractive red-veined leaves, which can transform a simple leaf salad.

Sorrel
Broad leaves with a sharp, slightly lemon flavour. Just a few leaves mixed with other salad leaves add interest to a simple salad. It can also be cooked like spinach.

Rocket
This is a popular addition to salad because of its pronounced, slightly peppery, fresh flavour as well as its firm texture and small, delicate and attractive leaves.

Chinese Leaves
This is a type of cabbage, with a light yet crunchy texture that is ideal for salads, particularly combined with bean sprouts, sesame seeds and grated ginger, coated with oriental-style dressings. Slice or shred the leaves across their width.

Watercress
Small, round, deep green leaves with a peppery, pungent flavour. It looks attractive mixed with paler salad leaves and contrasts well with tomatoes in salads or garnishes. Watercress can also be cooked in the same way as spinach, and added to soups, sauces and dressings.

Choosing and Storing Leaf Salads
All leaf vegetables should be bought very fresh and used as quickly as possible to enjoy them at their best and with maximum food value. They should be crisp, bright in colour and fresh-looking. Avoid limp, dry or yellowing leaves. Really fresh salad leaves can be stored successfully in the salad drawer of a refrigerator for 2–3 days. Whole heads of leaves keep better and for longer than prepared or cut leaves, which are best used on the day they are purchased.

How to Prepare Salad Vegetables

Preparing Leaves

Treat salad leaves gently because they bruise easily and can turn brown if overhandled.

1 Remove any damaged or coarse outer leaves and break the leaves from the stem.

2 Wash the leaves thoroughly in plenty of cold water to remove dirt or pesticide residues.

3 Drain the leaves and pat them dry on a clean tea towel or dry them in a salad spinner.

4 Most leaves should be torn, rather than cut with a knife, to ensure that the cells are left as undamaged as possible. Use a very sharp knife when shredding lettuce.

Preparing Avocado

Prepare avocado just before serving because the flesh discolours when allowed to stand, exposed to the air, for long.

1 Cut the avocado in half lengthways through the skin all the way around and into the stone. Hold one half in each hand, then twist the halves in opposite directions and pull them apart.

2 To remove the stone, tap the blade of a sharp knife into it and twist it out.

3 Peel the flesh or use a large spoon to scoop it out, keeping the spoon as close as possible to the skin.

4 Brush the flesh with lemon, lime or orange juice to prevent it from discolouring.

5 The avocado can be sliced lengthways or across. Cut across the slices to make dice.

Preparing Cucumber

1 Cucumber can be eaten with or without its peel. Use a vegetable peeler to peel cucumber thinly lengthways.

2 If you prefer to leave the peel on when slicing cucumber, the edges can be decorated by paring narrow grooves out of the peel using a canelle knife. Pare out the peel at regular intervals down the length of the cucumber. The slices will have a serrated edge.

3 Trim off the ends of the cucumber. To remove the seeds, cut the cucumber in half lengthways and use a teaspoon to scoop out the seeds.

4 To remove excess moisture and accentuate the flavour of cucumber, sprinkle it lightly with salt and leave to drain for about 20 minutes, then rinse and dry before use.

TIP • Grated cucumber mixed with natural yogurt makes a refreshing dip or dressing. Add chopped fresh mint or crushed garlic, to taste.

Layering Salads

Layering salads is a good method of advance preparation, for example when entertaining or for a picnic. First pour the salad dressing into a deep bowl. Top with layers of salad ingredients, such as sliced tomato, grated carrot, prepared salad leaves, cucumber and so on. Cover the bowl with clingfilm and chill until needed. To serve, invert the salad into a bowl or on to a deep platter, so that the dressing runs down to coat all the ingredients.

Perfect Dressings

The classic salad dressing, vinaigrette, is one of the most simple to make. The usual proportions are 3 parts oil to 1 part vinegar, but you can vary this to suit your own taste. If you use a straight-sided jar for mixing, you can see the proportions at a glance without having to measure them.

Choose good-quality extra virgin olive oil or use nut oil, such as walnut or hazelnut, for a different flavour. Flavoured oils, for example with chilli, garlic, lemon or herbs, bring variety to simple salads.

The choice of vinegar depends upon your own individual taste. Apart from classic white and red wine vinegars, sherry or balsamic vinegars have a more robust flavour. For a milder flavour, try cider vinegar. Salad vinegars flavoured with herbs, spices, fruits or even edible flowers can be used to enhance all kinds of salads.

Basic Vinaigrette or French Dressing

Makes: **125 ml/4 fl oz**
Preparation time: 5 minutes

6 tablespoons extra virgin olive oil
2 tablespoons red or white wine vinegar
1 teaspoon Dijon mustard
pinch of caster sugar
salt and pepper

Place all the ingredients in a screw-top jar, cover and shake well to combine.

VARIATIONS
Honey Citrus Dressing
Replace the wine vinegar with lemon or lime juice and add 1 teaspoon clear honey instead of the sugar.

Herb Dressing
Omit the mustard and add 2 tablespoons finely chopped fresh herbs, such as parsley, chives or chervil, or a mixture of herbs.

Warm Salad Dressings

Using a warm dressing is a particularly good way to add robust flavours that help to transform a simple salad of basic ingredients into a stunning dish. This simple dressing is a good example: it provides quite a pungent kick of flavours and tastes terrific with substantial salads – try it on Spinach, Avocado and Bacon Salad (see page 158), or over warm sliced duck with frisée and crunchy croûtons.

Warm Garlic and Chilli Dressing

Makes: **100 ml/3½ fl oz**
Preparation time: 10 minutes

5 tablespoons olive oil
1 small red chilli, deseeded and finely chopped
1 garlic clove, crushed
1 shallot, finely chopped
2 tablespoons lemon juice
salt and pepper

1 Heat the oil in a heavy-based pan. Add the chilli, garlic and shallot, then cook gently over a low heat, stirring, until the mixture is softened but not browned.
2 Whisk in the lemon juice and add salt and pepper to taste, then immediately pour the dressing over the salad and serve.

Spinach, Avocado and Bacon Salad

The secret of this favourite salad is to serve it while the bacon is still warm and the salad leaves still look and taste fresh.

Serves: **4–6**

Preparation time: 5 minutes

Cooking time: 8 minutes

1 ripe avocado, peeled and pitted
2 tablespoons lemon juice
500 g/1 lb young spinach leaves
1 small bunch spring onions, shredded into julienne strips
2 tablespoons sunflower oil
1 garlic clove, crushed
4 slices back bacon, rinded and chopped

1 Dice the avocado flesh and sprinkle with lemon juice to stop it discolouring.

2 Make sure the spinach leaves are thoroughly rinsed and dry, then tear into pieces and place in a serving bowl, together with the spring onions and avocado cubes.

3 Dry-fry the bacon with the garlic in a heavy-based frying pan until crisp and brown and all the fat has been released. Remove with a slotted spoon, drain on kitchen paper, then scatter over the spinach mixture.

4 Spoon Walnut Dressing over the salad, toss gently to coat and serve at once.

WALNUT DRESSING
Makes: **about 150 ml/¼ pint**

Preparation time: 10 minutes

3 tablespoons balsamic vinegar
1 teaspoon soft light brown sugar
1 teaspoon Dijon mustard
125 ml/4 fl oz walnut oil
1 tablespoon finely chopped walnuts
1 tablespoon chopped parsley or basil
salt and pepper

1 Combine the vinegar, sugar and mustard in a small bowl. Add salt and pepper to taste. Stir to mix, then gradually whisk in the walnut oil, using a balloon whisk.

2 Stir the chopped walnuts and herbs into the dressing and adjust the seasoning to taste.

Salade Niçoise

It is impossible to give a definitive recipe for Salade Niçoise since there is a lot of controversy over what can authentically be included. This version may be greeted with horror by traditionalists, but it is still a very good dish.

Serves: **2 as a main course**

Preparation time: 10 minutes

Cooking time: 15–18 minutes

about 250 g/8 oz small new potatoes, scrubbed, or medium potatoes, scrubbed and quartered
5 tablespoons virgin olive oil
2 tablespoons red wine vinegar
250 g/8 oz French beans
250 g/8 oz fresh tuna steak, cut into finger strips
2 garlic cloves, finely chopped
2 anchovy fillets, chopped
about 1½ teaspoons Dijon mustard
1 red pepper, charred, skinned, deseeded and thinly sliced
2 tablespoons capers
salt and pepper
lemon wedges, to serve (optional)

1 Steam the potatoes for 8–10 minutes, until just tender. Transfer to a serving bowl and toss gently with 1 tablespoon each of the oil and the vinegar and season to taste with salt and pepper.

2 Steam the French beans for 5–6 minutes until just tender. Set aside.

3 Heat 1 tablespoon of the oil in a non-stick frying pan. Add the tuna and sear evenly over a high heat. Add to the potato mixture.

4 Add the remaining oil to the frying pan, then stir in the garlic and anchovies for 30 seconds. Stir in the remaining vinegar and boil for about 1 minute. Stir in mustard to taste, then pour over the potato mixture. Add the pepper strips, beans, capers and more pepper. Toss gently, taste and adjust the flavourings if necessary, then serve the salad immediately with lemon wedges, if liked.

Fruit

Choosing Fruits

Make sure apricots, peaches and nectarines are ripe when you buy them, since they do not mature well after picking. Look for plump fruit with a rich colour and smooth skin. Avoid bruised or green-tinted fruit. Keep at cool room temperature or store in a polythene bag in the refrigerator for 2–3 days.

Plums, damsons and greengages are delicate and they ripen fast, so buy unblemished fruits and store them in the refrigerator for no longer than 2 days. They should be plump and firm, with a pleasant scent. Sweet, juicy dessert plums are usually larger than cooking varieties, which tend to be firm and less juicy.

Cherries should be plump, shiny and unblemished. The paler-skinned varieties tend to be sweeter; the dark ones are usually more tart in flavour. If possible, taste before buying to check. Unwashed, they will keep for several days in the refrigerator.

Fresh dates should be plump and moist, with smooth, unwrinkled skin. Ripe dates are deep brown in colour; unripe fruit are more golden in colour.

Apples, Pears and Orchard Fruit

These include apples, pears, crab apples and quinces. Look for good-quality fruit that is clean and unblemished.

Many dessert apples are at their peak flavour when smaller in size, particularly Cox's Orange Pippin, Egremont Russet, Discovery, Spartan and Worcester Pearmain. It is best to buy dessert apples in small quantities and often, since they become soft and woolly textured when kept in warm conditions. However, many varieties, particularly Bramley cooking apples, will keep for months in a dark, moist, cool, frost-proof store, but to be stored successfully, the fruit must be absolutely perfect and laid out so that the individual apples to not touch each other.

Pears are fragile and they bruise easily, so treat them gently. They do not keep well in domestic storage conditions, so it is best to buy them in small amounts. Unripe pears ripen in a warm, draught-free place, such as an airing cupboard, within 2–3 days.

Stone Fruit

Includes apricots, peaches, nectarines, plums, damsons, greengages, cherries and dates.

Berries and Soft Fruit

This group consists of strawberries, raspberries, blackberries, redcurrants, blackcurrants, whitecurrants, blueberries, cranberries, gooseberries and loganberries.

All berry fruits should be plump and glossy with a good colour. Use these within 1–2 days, since most will not keep well. Strawberries should have fresh, green calyxes (their tops). Avoid damaged or mouldy fruit and check by looking underneath punnets for signs of lots of juice from squashed fruits. To keep soft berries fresh, line a shallow tray with kitchen paper, and turn them out on to it in a single layer.

Cover the tray loosely with clingfilm and place in the refrigerator.

Citrus Fruit

These include oranges, lemons, limes, grapefruit, kumquats, pomelos, uglis and small citrus, such as tangerines, mandarins and minneolas. Citrus fruits should be firm and unblemished with a good colour. They should feel heavy for their size, since this indicates that they are full of juice. Many varieties of tangerine have loose, puffy skins, which is not a sign of poor quality – these are easy to peel and are very good for picnics, packed lunches and no-mess snacks.

If you plan to use citrus rinds, you may prefer to buy unwaxed fruits, which have not been coated to keep their skins fresh. If not, scrub the fruit well before using the rind. Citrus fruit yields more juice when warm, so either roll the fruit in your hands or heat it in the microwave on high (100% power) for 30 seconds before squeezing it.

Exotic Fruit

Bananas, mangoes, guavas, papaya, figs, kiwifruit, passion fruit, carambola (star fruit), lychees, pomegranates, pineapples, tamarillo and persimmons (Sharon fruit) all belong to this group. Many types of exotic fruit are picked unripe and stored under controlled conditions so that they ripen slowly. Once ripened, many are fragile, so check for bruised or damaged fruits before buying and treat them with care.

Colour is not necessarily a sign of ripeness – while some mangoes, for instance, remain green when ripe, others will have a red-blushed skin even when unripe. The best test is to apply gentle pressure – the flesh should

yield slightly when ripe. The aroma is also a useful indicator of ripeness, since ripe mango have a delicate perfume.

To test pineapple for condition, gently pull a leaf – it should pull out easily when ripe.

Melons and Grapes

Water melon, honeydew, charentais, galia, ogen and piel de sapo (emerald sugar melon) are all types of melon. They should feel heavy for their size and have a pleasant, sweet scent. Press gently at the opposite end to the stalk to check condition – the skin should give just

slightly when ripe. Unripe melons can be ripened at room temperature, but once ripe, keep them in a cool, airy place. If you store melon in the refrigerator, wrap it thoroughly in clingfilm to prevent its distinct scent from tainting other foods.

Grapes are often sold unripe, so taste one before buying, if possible. Choose a bunch with grapes of equal size and with a slight bloom. Over-ripe grapes will fall off the bunch easily and the stems will be brown and shrivelled. Use grapes quickly or store them in a polythene bag in the salad drawer of the refrigerator for up to a week.

How to Prepare Fruit

Peeling and Segmenting Citrus Fruit

1 Use a sharp knife to cut single slices off the top and bottom of the fruit.

2 Stand the fruit on a board and cut off all the peel, slicing downwards in sections. Remove all the white pith and outer membrane from the fruit with the peel.

3 Hold the fruit over a bowl to catch any juice. Keeping the knife blade away from you, cut between the membranes and the flesh of each segment, easing out the segments as you go round the fruit.

Citrus Fruit Garnishes

Citrus fruit, particularly lemons and limes, make particularly useful fresh and simple garnishes and decorations for all kinds of sweet and savoury dishes.

1 A zester is the best tool for cutting fine strips of citrus rind to scatter over sweet or savoury dishes. If the strips are not to be used immediately, blanch them in boiling water for a

few seconds, then refresh in cold water. Drain and place in a covered container to prevent the shreds from shrivelling.

2 To make julienne strips of citrus rind, use a canelle knife to cut channels down the rind. For long spirals of zest, cut in a spiral around and down the fruit, then twist the strip of rind into a spiral shape.

3 To make decorative slices, use a canelle knife to score channels down the length of the fruit at equal intervals. Then slice the fruit in the usual way.

4 To make twists, thinly slice the fruit. Make a cut from the centre of each slice to the outer edge. Twist the edges of the cut apart in opposite directions, to stand the slice in a twist or 'S' shape.

5 To cut wedges, halve the fruit lengthways and then cut each half lengthways into wedges. Trim a little off the centre ridge along each wedge to remove excess membrane and allow the juice to be squeezed out easily.

Making Apple Leaves

Apple leaves make an attractive garnish, and they are easier to make than their complicated appearance suggests.

1 Cut a long, narrow 'V'-shaped notch, or wedge, lengthways into the side of a dessert apple. Cut again on either side of the first cuts to make a larger wedge. Leave the pieces of apple in place when cut.
2 Continue cutting wedges, each slightly larger than the last, to make about 5–6 layers.
3 Lift out the pieces all together from the apple. Push each piece up slightly to reveal part of the one below and create a leaf effect.

How to Prepare Mango

To find out which way the stone lies in a mango, place the fruit on the worktop and the fruit will naturally lie such that the stone is parallel to the worktop.

Hold the mango with the narrow side down and cut a thick slice from one side of the fruit, as close to the stone as possible. Repeat on the other side, then cut off any flesh remaining around the stone. Either peel each large slice before dicing or slicing the flesh or make a mango hedgehog.

Making a Mango Hedgehog

Prepare the mango as above, giving two large slices with peel on. Use the tip of a knife to score deep lines in a diamond pattern into the flesh of each slice. Make the cuts about 1 cm/½ inch apart and take care not to cut right through the skin of the mango. Gently push up each slice from the skin side, so that the cut flesh pops up in a squared pattern, resembling a hedgehog.

How to Prepare Pineapple

Pineapple can be simply cut into wedges and served with the skin on, but if you plan to use the flesh on its own, the peel, spines and core have to be removed.

1 Trim off the base and top of the fruit, removing the leaves.
2 Stand the pineapple on a board and cut off the peel in long slices down the length of the fruit, removing as little flesh as possible.
3 To remove the sharp, brown eyes or spines from the flesh, use a small, sharp knife to cut long, spiralling grooves around the fruit, following the natural lines of the eyes.
4 Cut the pineapple across into slices. Remove the core from each slice by stamping it out using a small, round cutter.
5 To cut wedges or dice the flesh, cut the fruit lengthways into quarters. Cut away the tough line of core down the length of each wedge.

How to Prepare Melons

Melon Wedges

Cut slim wedges lengthways into the fruit, stem to base. Scoop out the seeds. Cut between the flesh and the skin, but leave the flesh in place, then cut it across to make bite-sized pieces. Push the melon pieces out slightly in alternate directions, overhanging the edges of the skin at the sides of the wedges, for an attractive presentation.

Melon Baskets

Cut slim slices from the base and top of each melon, so that each half will sit firmly. Use a short, sharp knife to make deep cuts in a zig-zag pattern all around the middle and into the centre of the fruit. Pull the 2 halves apart and scoop out the seeds. Serve the melon as it is or scoop out the flesh and mix it with soft fruit, then pile the fruit back in the basket halves. For small, single-portion melons, cut a thick slice from the top of the fruit and scoop out the seeds.

Melon Balls

Use a melon baller tool to scoop deep into the flesh and turn it full circle to scoop out neat balls of flesh. For an impressive yet simple dessert, try mixing together balls of different types and colours of melon, such as galia, charentais and watermelon.

Marinating Fruit

Any ripe, tender fruit, particularly soft fruits such as strawberries or raspberries, are enhanced by gentle marinating to bring out their flavour to the full. Sweetly-scented muscat wines, such as *Beaumes de Venise*, or fruit liqueurs, such as cassis, are the perfect choice. If you use stronger spirits, such as rum, brandy or kirsch, add only a small amount to moisten the fruit, and balance the flavour with a sprinkling of sugar.

Hull the fruit and place in a bowl. Sprinkle liberally with enough of the chosen wine or liqueur. Cover and chill for 2–3 hours, turning once. Scatter with sprigs of fresh mint or borage to serve.

Baking Apples

Baked apples make an economical and substantial hot winter pudding. Bramleys are the best choice for this method – choose fruits that are even in size and not too large for a single portion.

1 Wash and dry the apples and remove the cores with a corer or small knife.
2 Run a sharp knife around the middle of the apple to slit the skin and prevent it from bursting during cooking. Alternatively, use a canelle knife to score a line around the apple or at intervals downwards through the skin.
3 Place the apples in a shallow ovenproof dish and spoon the chosen filling into the central hole left by the core. If you do not want to add a filling, just sprinkle in caster sugar and cinnamon and dot with butter.
4 Sprinkle with lemon juice and bake in a preheated oven at 180°C/350°F/Gas Mark 4 for 45–60 minutes or until tender.

Fillings for Baked Apples

Mincemeat or jam
Chopped walnuts and dates
Chopped ready-to-eat dried apricots and almond paste
Crumbled ratafia biscuits or ginger nuts and flaked almonds
Cranberries and maple syrup

Poaching Fruit

Poaching is an excellent way to make a sophisticated dessert from simple fruit. The poaching liquid may be sugar and water, fruit juice, such as apple or cranberry, red or white wine or cider. To poach whole pears in wine, choose firm fruit, such as Williams or Conference, which will endure long, slow simmering for the flavours to develop, without breaking up.

Poached Pears in Wine

Serves: **6**
Preparation time: about 15 minutes
Cooking time: about 1¾–2 hours

6 large very firm pears
50 g/2 oz caster sugar
500 ml/17 fl oz red or white wine
1 vanilla pod
thinly pared strip of lemon rind
1 cinnamon stick
2 teaspoons arrowroot

1 Peel the pears thinly, leaving the stalks on. Trim a thin slice from the base of each so that it stands upright.
2 Place the sugar, wine and vanilla pod in a flameproof casserole and heat gently, stirring, until almost boiling.
3 Add the pears, then the lemon rind and cinnamon. Bring to a gentle simmer, then cover the casserole and simmer very gently over a very low heat, for about 1 hour. Alternatively, cook in a preheated oven at 120°C/250°F/Gas Mark ½.
4 Gently turn the pears in the syrup, then poach them for a further 45–60 minutes or until very tender, turning occasionally.
5 Carefully lift the pears from the syrup and discard the flavourings. Mix the arrowroot with a little cold water to make a smooth paste, then stir it into the hot syrup.
6 Bring to the boil, stirring, then stir for 1 minute and remove from the heat. Do not cook the syrup any longer since the arrowroot thins slightly with long simmering. Pour the syrup over the pears. Serve warm or cold.

Exotic Fruit Salad

A fresh fruit salad is the perfect way to cleanse the palate and end a meal. It takes a little time to prepare, but both looks impressive and tastes wonderful.

Serves: **4–6**

Preparation time: 5–10 minutes

Cooking time: 5 minutes

2 tablespoons clear honey
125 ml/4 fl oz water
thinly pared rind and juice of 1 lemon
2 bananas
1 small pineapple
2 oranges
2 kiwifruit, peeled and thinly sliced
1 mango, peeled, pitted and cut into cubes
125 g/4 oz strawberries, hulled and halved
1 small Charentais or Galia melon, peeled and
  cut into cubes or scooped into balls
ground cinnamon
mint sprigs, to decorate

1 Place the honey, water and lemon rind in a small saucepan. Bring to the boil over a low heat, simmer for 2 minutes, then strain and set aside to cool. Stir in the lemon juice.

2 Slice the bananas into diagonal slices and place in a bowl. Pour over the lemon syrup and stir to coat the fruit completely.

3 Peel the pineapple with a sharp knife, remove the eyes and cut the flesh into sections, discarding the central core.

4 Peel the oranges, removing all the pith, and divide into segments. Add to the bowl with the pineapple, kiwifruit, mango, strawberries and melon. Mix carefully, but thoroughly.

5 Turn into a serving bowl and chill until required. Sprinkle with cinnamon and decorate with mint sprigs before serving.

FOOD FACT • For advice on preparing pineapple and mango, and segmenting oranges, see pages 166–168.

Summer Pudding

This classic, glamorous dessert lives up to its name. You can even use frozen fruit and still evoke the feeling of warm sunshine at any time of year.

Serves: **8**

Preparation time: 5 minutes, plus chilling

Cooking time: 10–15 minutes

250 g/8 oz redcurrants
125 g/4 oz caster sugar
250 g/8 oz strawberries
250 g/8 oz raspberries
8 slices white bread, crusts removed
redcurrant sprigs, to garnish
whipped or pouring cream, to serve

1 Place the redcurrants in a heavy-based saucepan with the sugar. Cook over a low heat, stirring occasionally, for 10–15 minutes, until tender. Add the strawberries and raspberries and set aside to cool. Strain the fruit, reserving the juice.

2 Cut 3 circles of bread the same diameter as a 900 ml/1½ pint pudding basin. Shape the remaining bread to fit around the sides of the basin. Soak all the bread in the reserved fruit juice.

3 Line the base of the basin with one of the circles, then arrange the shaped bread around the sides. Pour in half the fruit and place another circle of bread on top. Cover with the remaining fruit, then top with the remaining bread circle.

4 Cover with a saucer small enough to fit inside the basin and put a 500 g/1 lb weight on top. Set aside in the refrigerator overnight.

5 Turn on to a serving plate, pour over any remaining fruit juice and garnish with a few reducurrant sprigs arranged on top of the pudding in the centre. Serve with whipped or pouring cream.

Herbs and
Spices

Types of Herbs

types, including an attractive purple-leafed variety. The leaves have a strong, sweet and spicy scent and pleasantly intense flavour, with overtones of aniseed. The leaves bruise easily and should be shredded rather than chopped, then added at the end of cooking, since the flavour is destroyed by heating.

Coriander
Delicate, bright-green leaves with a strongly aromatic and pungent flavour that complements chicken, fish, curries, rice and tomatoes. Coriander is widely used in Thai, Chinese, South American and Indian cooking.

Lemon Grass
This is a tropical grass that has a distinctive perfumed lemon flavour. It is widely used in Thai, Indonesian and Malaysian dishes. The outer leaves can be infused for flavour, but should be removed before serving. The tender centre can be finely sliced and sprinkled into dishes, particularly using poultry or fish.

Mint
There are hundreds of different varieties of mint, but the most common type used in cooking is spearmint. Its sweet, refreshing flavour is traditional with lamb, new potatoes

Chervil
A delicate herb that is related to parsley, this is particularly good in egg or cheese dishes and salads. Its feathery, tender leaves are a fresh green colour and have a slightly aniseed flavour. Add it towards the end of cooking.

Chives
These long, slim, reed-like stems are from a plant related to the lily. They have a distinct onion flavour that complements eggs, cheese, soups, tomatoes, fish, chicken and salads. Chives are best snipped with scissors and added late in the cooking process, or sprinkled over as a garnish.

Dill
Related to parsley, this herb has delicate green fronds with a sweet, anise-like scent and flavour. Dill is good with fish, eggs, cheese and vegetables, and makes an attractive garnish.

Tarragon
These long, elegant, fresh green leaves are from a plant belonging to the sunflower family.

French tarragon has the finest, most delicate flavour, with an anise accent. The chopped leaves complement fish, chicken, veal, lamb, eggs, salads, soups and sauces.

Basil
Used in many Mediterranean dishes, particularly pesto, with tomato, pizzas and salads. The leaves of standard basil are a bright, rich green but there are 150 different

and peas, but it is also excellent in salads, soups and drinks. When mixed with yogurt, mint makes a lively contrast to spicy dishes.

Parsley

One of the best-known herbs, parsley is available in curly-leafed or flat-leafed (Italian) varieties. It has a fresh green colour and sweet, mild flavour that enlivens most savoury dishes. Use it lavishly in fish, poultry and meat dishes, and with vegetables and salads.

Rosemary

The firm, needle-shaped leaves of this fragrant evergreen shrub have a distinctive, pungent flavour with overtones of pine-wood. Rosemary is particularly good with lamb and useful for marinades and barbecued meats, especially when combined with garlic.

Sage

These strongly flavoured, silvery-green leaves are from an evergreen shrub, native to the Mediterranean. It has a powerful, slightly musty flavour that has an affinity with fatty foods, especially pork, veal and cheese. Try using it with sausages, tomatoes, potatoes and nut roasts.

Thyme

Common thyme is one of the most widely used of the many varieties of thyme that grow throughout the Mediterranean and Asia. It is a small, woody plant with tiny grey-green leaves that have a strong, fragrant aroma. It is ideal for long-cooked casseroles or stews and is a classic flavouring in French cassoulets and rich, meaty daubes, as well as in Irish Stew and Lancashire Hotpot.

Bay

These oval-shaped, dark green, firm leaves have a strong, distinctive, slightly astringent flavour which is good in most savoury dishes. It is often used in stocks, marinades and sauces, and is particularly useful in casseroles since its flavour increases with cooking time. Bay can be used fresh or dried. One leaf is usually enough to give a subtle, but quite distinct, flavour.

Marjoram and Oregano

These are very closely related. Both have a fragrant, slightly spicy flavour. Marjoram is delicate and sweet but oregano, also known as wild marjoram, is more pungent. Both are widely used in Mediterranean cooking, and are good with poultry, meat, eggs, cheese, in stuffings and on pizzas.

How to Use Herbs

Chopping Herbs

1 Wash the herbs and dry on a clean tea towel or kitchen paper.

2 Hold the leaves together firmly in a bunch and, using your knuckles as a guide, slice through the leaves with a straight-bladed, sharp knife to chop the herbs coarsely.

3 Hold the knife handle with one hand and the tip down firmly on the chopping board with the other hand, then use a rocking action to chop the herbs finely.

Using Scissors to Cut Herbs

To chop a small amount of herbs, such as parsley, trim off the stalks and put the leaves in a small measuring jug. Use scissors, blades downwards, to chop the herbs. Use scissors to snip herbs, such as chives, directly onto food.

Making a Bouquet Garni

This is simply a small bundle of herbs tied together with fine string or heavy cotton. Add to stocks, soups or stews to infuse the liquid with the flavour of the herbs, then remove the bundle before serving. Tie the herbs firmly by their stems. If you prefer, the herbs may be tied into a bundle in a small square of muslin.

Traditionally, the basic bouquet garni includes a fresh bay leaf, sprig of fresh thyme and 2–3 sprigs of fresh parsley. This can be varied according to the dish it is to flavour. Add a sprig of fresh rosemary for lamb, a fresh sage

sprig for pork, a sprig of celery leaves or piece of celery stick for beef, or a strip of thinly pared lemon rind with a sprig of dill or fennel for fish or chicken.

Garnishing with Herbs

Fresh herbs are an invaluable and easy garnish. Before chopping herbs for use in any dish, it is worth reserving a few of the choicest sprigs for garnishing.

Pick off the prettiest leaves and arrange in a single layer on a tray lined with kitchen paper. Spray lightly with water, cover with clingfilm and they will stay fresh in the refrigerator for hours, ready to use for garnishing the dish at the last moment.

Frosted mint leaves make a pretty decoration for cold desserts. Wash and dry the sprigs, then use a small paintbrush to paint the leaves lightly with egg white. Sprinkle with caster sugar, shaking off the excess. Leave to dry on a sheet of kitchen or non-stick baking paper.

Herb-Flavoured Oils and Vinegars

Commercial herb-flavoured oils and vinegars are expensive, but they are easy to make at home. Use any fresh herbs and add sprigs to a bottle of good-quality olive oil or to wine vinegar, sherry vinegar or cider vinegar. Fresh, clean sprigs of rosemary, thyme or lengths of chives can be used. If you want additional flavour, add a whole chilli, a twist of lemon or orange rind and a few peppercorns. Cover tightly and allow to stand for at least 2 weeks before using.

Basil Oil

Not only is this an excellent way to make a fragrant cooking oil, but it is also a very successful way to preserve basil for winter

months. Pack leaves into a screw-top bottle or jar and pour in olive oil to cover them. Leave undisturbed for 1–2 weeks. The oil can be used to make salad dressings or drizzle a little into soups or simple savoury dishes before serving.

Making Herb Butters

Prepare 2 tablespoons finely chopped fresh herbs, such as parsley, mint, chives or chervil. Mix into 125 g/4 oz unsalted butter at room temperature and add a squeeze of lemon or lime juice. Beat well with a wooden spoon or electric mixer to combine evenly.

Turn the butter out on to a piece of clingfilm or non-stick baking paper. Fold the clingfilm or paper over the butter and shape it into a roll about 5 cm/2 inches in diameter. Wrap and chill until firm. Unwrap and slice with a knife.

Alternatively, turn the butter out onto clingfilm or non-stick baking paper and spread it out evenly. Place another sheet on top and press lightly with a rolling pin to an even thickness of about 5 mm/¼ inch thick. Chill until firm, then use small cutters to stamp out shapes.

How to Dry Herbs

Air Drying

Tie very fresh summer herbs in small bundles with string and hang them in a cool, dry, airy place for 1-2 weeks until dry and crisp. Once dry, store in airtight containers to retain flavour.

Microwave Drying

Arrange small sprigs or leaves in a single, even layer on a round platter lined with kitchen paper. Place a small dish of water in the centre and microwave on high (100% power) for about 30 seconds. Repeat in 30-second bursts until the herbs are crisp and dry. Cool for a few minutes before storing in an airtight container.

Salmon Steaks in Fresh Coriander Sauce

Coriander has a natural affinity with fish, providing a delicate addition to the flavour rather than overwhelming it.

Serves: **4**

Preparation time: 10 minutes

Cooking time: 40 minutes

Oven temperature: 190°C/375°F/Gas Mark 5

4 salmon steaks, 175–250 g/6–8 oz each
125 g/4 oz unsalted butter, plus extra for greasing
½ onion, finely chopped
1 carrot, cut into matchstick strips
1 garlic clove, finely chopped
1 bay leaf
1 tablespoon dry vermouth (optional)
125 ml/4 fl oz Fish Stock (see page 39)
1 bunch of coriander, finely chopped
125 ml/4 fl oz double cream
1–2 tablespoons lemon juice
sea salt and pepper
freshly cooked vegetables, such as new potatoes and French beans, to serve
TO GARNISH
lime slices
flat-leafed parsley sprigs

1 Rinse the salmon steaks in cold water, pat dry and season with salt and pepper.

2 Melt half the butter in a small frying pan. Add the onion and carrot and sauté over a low heat for 4–5 minutes. Add the garlic and cook for a further 2 minutes.

3 Pour into a shallow ovenproof dish, add the bay leaf, then arrange the fish on top in a single layer. Sprinkle with vermouth, if using, then with the fish stock. Cover with buttered foil and bake in a preheated oven, 190°C/375°F/Gas Mark 5, for 20–25 minutes, depending on the thickness of the fish. It should just flake easily when tested with a fork (see page 91).

4 Remove the fish to a warmed serving plate and keep warm.

5 Strain the cooking juices into a clean pan and boil vigorously for 1–2 minutes to reduce.

6 Add half the remaining butter, the coriander and the cream, and simmer for 4–5 minutes, until slightly thickened. Add the lemon juice, stir for 1 minute, then add the remaining butter and whisk until smooth and glossy. Adjust the seasoning, if necessary, then pour over the fish, garnish with the lime slices and flat-leafed parsley and serve with vegetables.

Tarragon Chicken

Chicken and tarragon is a classic combination, but make sure that you use French tarragon with its aromatic, slightly aniseed flavour, rather than the Russian variety.

Serves: **5–6**

Preparation time: 5 minutes

Cooking time: 1 hour 35 minutes

1.5–1.75 kg/3–3½ lb chicken
1 onion
1 carrot
1 bay leaf
3 parsley sprigs
3 thyme sprigs, plus extra to garnish
12 black peppercorns
sea salt and pepper
tarragon sprigs, to garnish
mixed-leaf salad, to serve
SAUCE
25 g/1 oz butter
2 tablespoons plain flour
150 ml/¼ pint double cream
3 tablespoons chopped tarragon

1 Put the chicken in a saucepan just large enough to hold it. Add just enough cold water almost to cover it, then remove the chicken.

2 Put the onion and carrot in the pan, together with the bay leaf, parsley, thyme, peppercorns and sea salt to taste. Bring to the boil, lower the heat, cover and simmer for 30 minutes.

3 Return the chicken to the pan, bring back to the boil, cover and simmer over a very low heat for about 1 hour, or until the juices run clear (see page 112). Remove the chicken and carve the meat into neat slices. Arrange the slices on a shallow serving dish, cover with foil and keep warm while you make the sauce.

4 If the pan was only just big enough to hold the chicken, you should have a small amount of good stock. Otherwise, reduce it by boiling vigorously to 300 ml/½ pint. Strain and skim off as much fat as possible from the surface.

5 Melt the butter in a small saucepan, add the flour and cook, stirring constantly, for 1 minute. Gradually stir in the strained stock. Stir until thoroughly blended, then add the cream. Simmer gently for 4 minutes, season with salt and pepper to taste and stir in the chopped tarragon.

6 Pour a little of the sauce over the chicken slices and serve the remainder in a sauceboat. Garnish with tarragon sprigs and serve with a mixed-leaf salad.

VARIATION • Use 3 tablespoons chopped dill in place of the tarragon.

Types of Spices

dishes, particularly ham or onion, cakes, biscuits, pickles, mulled wine and fruit.

Ginger
This popular spice is the underground stem of a tropical iris-like plant. It has a warm, sweet, citrus-like aroma and hot, spicy flavour. Peel and chop or grate the fresh root. Add ground (dried) ginger or prepared fresh root ginger to curries, meat dishes, cakes and bakes, pickles and oriental dishes.

Nutmeg and Mace
These come from an evergreen tree native to the Spice Islands. Nutmeg is the hard, brown seed and mace is its lacy orange covering. Both have an aromatic, sweet, warm, rich flavour, but nutmeg is the strongest. Available whole or ground, nutmeg is best freshly grated. They complement beef, seafood, vegetables, biscuits, cakes and milk puddings.

Saffron
The dried vibrant golden-red stigmas of a crocus make one of the most expensive spices. The distinctive flavour is delicate and honey-like. It is the classic spice for paella and risotto, and is used in baking. Saffron is good with fish, chicken, curries and potato dishes.

Cardamom
These little pale-green pods contain tiny brown-black seeds. They are the dried, unripened fruit of a perennial plant of the ginger family. Their flavour is highly aromatic and citrus-like, resembling eucalyptus. It is available ground, but you will get the best flavour by crushing the pods with a pestle and mortar. It is used in curries, rice dishes, Middle Eastern sweets and pastries.

Cayenne Pepper
A very powerful hot spice, made from ground dried hot red chillies. It has a beautiful bright

Allspice
These dark red-brown berries are from a tree native to the West Indies. The flavour of allspice resembles a mixture of cinnamon, nutmeg and cloves. Used whole or ground, it has an affinity with poultry, beef and pork. It is also very good with cheese or in pickles, cakes and bakes.

Caraway
These curved, creamy-brown seeds are from a plant related to parsley. They have a warm, pungent, slightly bitter flavour with overtones of anise. Caraway is popular in German, Austrian and Hungarian cookery with potatoes, cabbage, goulash, cheese, breads and cakes.

Star Anise
An attractive star-shaped fruit pod containing shiny brown seeds with a pungent anise

flavour. Use sparingly, either whole or ground in Chinese dishes, meat, poultry, casseroles, stir-fries, fruit compôtes and cakes.

Cinnamon
The curled, dried bark of a tropical evergreen tree of the laurel family, cinnamon's warm, sweet, woody flavour is very versatile. Infuse sticks of bark in mulled wines or with poached fruit, or add ground cinnamon to meat dishes and vegetables or cakes and bakes. Ground cinnamon is the perfect topping for a frothy drink of hot chocolate – or use a cinnamon stick to stir the hot drink.

Cloves
These are the dried flower buds of an evergreen tree native to the Spice Islands. They have a strong, sweet, pungent flavour and can be used whole or ground to complement meat

orange colour, but should be used only very sparingly to flavour meat, vegetable, egg and cheese dishes.

Coriander
The light brown seeds of the coriander plant have a very different flavour from the leaves. Their flavour is mild, sweet and pungent, with a burnt orange-like taste. Use whole or ground in Indian or Middle Eastern dishes, with stewed fruit, in pickles, cakes and biscuits.

Cumin
These yellowish-brown seeds of a plant related to cow parsley are available whole or ground. Cumin has a strong, earthy aroma and slightly bitter flavour. It is good with chicken, lamb, cheese, vegetables, curries, breads and in Mexican dishes.

Fennel Seeds
These yellow-brown seeds are the dried ripe fruits of the fennel plant. Their flavour is sweet and slightly anise-like. Use with fish, pork, potatoes, eggs, cheese, pickles and apples.

Mustard
White, black and brown mustard seeds vary in strength – black are the strongest. Used whole or ground, the clean, fresh aroma and warming flavour is useful in savoury cooking, particularly with pork, veal, rabbit, fish, curries, vegetables, cheese and pickles.

Paprika
This deep-red spice is ground from dried sweet peppers, originally from South America. It is often used for colour and garnish. The subtle, earthy pepper flavour of paprika is very good with pork and chicken dishes, vegetables, potatoes, cheese and eggs. It is an essential ingredient in Hungarian goulash.

Peppercorns
The berries of a tropical vine. Black peppercorns are the whole green berries that blacken when dried; white are ripe berries with the outer skin removed before drying; and milder green peppercorns are picked unripe, then dried. The warm, pungent aroma of pepper is enhanced by heating. Pepper complements all savoury dishes.

Turmeric
This brilliant-yellow powder is made from the ground underground stem of a rhizome related to ginger. It has a pungent, earthy flavour which is appreciated in curries, rice, pickles and creamy sauces.

Vanilla
Long, slender, black pods from a climbing orchid native to the tropical forests of Central America. The sweet, slightly smoky flavour and aroma of vanilla is highly prized in sweet dishes. The pods can be used several times to infuse liquids. Good-quality vanilla extract is the only alternative. Add to cakes, puddings, ices, cream desserts and custards.

How to Use Spices

Using Fresh Ginger Root

Grating

The easiest, quickest way to prepare root ginger is to grate it. There is no need to peel it: just trim off any tough areas or dried parts and grate the root on a fine food grater. Most of the skin will be left behind, and the juicy flesh is ready to use.

Using Whole Ginger

Whole pieces of ginger root are excellent infused in preserves, but to get the best flavour, you should always bruise the ginger first to release the juices. The most effective way to do this is by placing the root on a solid worktop and hitting it firmly with the base of a heavy pan.

Using Vanilla Pods

To infuse milk, cream or other liquids with a delicate vanilla flavour, add a vanilla pod to the liquid and heat gently for a few minutes until almost boiling. Cover, remove from the heat and leave to infuse for 10–20 minutes. Remove the pod, rinse it dry, then store it in an airtight container ready for use again.

For a stronger vanilla flavour, split the pod lengthways and scrape out the tiny black oily seeds to add to the dish.

Vanilla sugar is useful for adding a subtle flavour to delicate dishes. Store a whole vanilla pod in a jar of caster sugar, and the sugar will absorb the flavour of the spice ready for use in desserts and puddings.

Enhancing Spice Flavours

All spices are best when very fresh, so only buy them in small amounts and keep them in airtight containers in a cool, dark place, away

from any powerful heat source, such as a cooker or a radiator.

Dry-roasting Spices

Gentle heating mellows the flavour of many spices, making them taste less 'raw' in dishes. This is best done with whole spices, before grinding. Heat a dry, heavy-based frying pan, add the spices and stir over a moderate heat for 2–5 minutes until lightly and evenly browned. Cool before grinding.

Grinding Spices

Freshly ground or crushed spices have the most flavour. If possible, grind your own spices in a mortar with a pestle. However, a spice mill or a coffee grinder (kept just for spices) is more practical for larger quantities.

Frying Spices

When adding spices to savoury dishes, such as curries, it improves their flavour if you fry the spices in oil before adding other ingredients. This releases their flavour and helps the spice to permeate the other ingredients. Fry whole spices first, separately from ground spices. Stir continously over a fairly high heat to brown the spices lightly, but do not burn them or they will taste bitter.

How to Make Spice Pastes

Spice pastes are convenient but they can be expensive to buy, so it is worth making your own. This is a basic paste: vary the mix to your own taste or for different types of curry.

Basic Garam Masala Curry Paste

Makes: **about 75 g/3 oz**
Preparation time: 10 minutes
Cooking time: 5–7 minutes

25 g/1 oz coriander seeds
20 g/¾ oz cumin seeds

1 tablespoon black peppercorns
1 tablespoon cloves
5 cm/2 inch piece of cinnamon stick
6 green cardamoms
1 teaspoon fennel seeds
2 dried bay leaves
50 ml/2 fl oz white wine vinegar
50 ml/2 fl oz vegetable oil, plus extra for storing

1 Dry-roast all the spices separately, then cool and grind them separately to a powder. Grind the bay leaves to a powder. Mix together, then add the vinegar, adding a little extra, if necessary, to make a smooth paste.
2 Heat the oil in a heavy-based pan. Add the spice paste and stir-fry for 3–4 minutes, until most of the moisture has evaporated.
3 Remove from the heat and leave to stand for 2–3 minutes – the oil should float to the surface. Spoon the paste into a sterilised jar. Cover with a little oil and seal.

Making Peppered Steaks

1 Rub sirloin or fillet steaks with a cut clove of garlic and brush them lightly with oil.
2 Allow about ½ teaspoon each of black and white peppercorns for each steak. Coarsely crush the equal quantities of white and black peppercorns in a mortar with a pestle – they must not be too fine.
3 Press the peppercorns into the surface of the steaks to coat evenly on both sides.
4 Cover with clingfilm and chill for at least 1 hour to allow the flavour to penetrate.
5 Sprinkle the steaks lightly with salt and dry-fry them in a ridged pan or griddle, turning once (see cooking times for steak, page 128).

Stir-fried Duck with Ginger and Vegetables

Because duck breast, like chicken breast, is so tender, it requires very little cooking and therefore lends itself particularly well to stir-frying. This dish goes well with boiled rice or noodles.

Serves: **4**

Preparation time: 15 minutes

Cooking time: 8–10 minutes

2 boneless, skinless duck breasts, weighing about 500 g/1 lb in total
1 red pepper
1 green pepper, deseeded
1 large carrot
1 cm/½ inch piece of fresh root ginger
8 spring onions
125 g/4 oz bean sprouts
2 tablespoons sunflower oil
SAUCE
2 garlic cloves, crushed
2 tablespoons cornflour
1 tablespoon Szechuan seasoning
2 tablespoons dark brown sugar
1 teaspoon ground ginger
4 tablespoons soy sauce
2 tablespoons sherry
600 ml/1 pint Chicken or Vegetable Stock (see page 39)

1 Cut the duck into strips about 1 cm/½ inch wide.

2 Cut the pepper into strips about 4 cm/1½ inches long and 3 mm/⅛ inch thick. Cut the carrot to a similar size and shape. Thinly slice the ginger. Cut the spring onions into 4 cm/1½ inch lengths.

3 Combine all the ingredients for the sauce in a large measuring jug.

4 Heat the oil in a preheated wok or large, heavy-based frying pan. Add the duck and stir-fry for about 3 minutes, until it is just beginning to colour. Add all the vegetables and continue to stir-fry for a further few minutes, tossing everything together in the pan.

5 Stir the sauce to make sure it is well blended, then pour it into the pan. Bring to the boil and cook for a few minutes, stirring constantly to combine the flavours while the sauce is cooking and thickening. Once thickened, serve immediately.

Chicken Tagine with Vegetables and Chick Peas

A tagine is a traditional Moroccan spiced stew. For a really authentic flavour, serve with couscous.

Serves: **4**

Preparation time: 8 minutes

Cooking time: about 1¼ hours

2 tablespoons olive oil

1 Spanish onion, chopped

4 garlic cloves, crushed

1 fresh red chilli, deseeded and finely chopped

1 tablespoon grated fresh root ginger

1½ teaspoons ground cumin

1½ teaspoons ground coriander

1 teaspoon ground allspice

4 chicken legs

750 ml/1¼ pints Chicken Stock (see page 39)

1 red pepper, deseeded and sliced

1 courgette, sliced

2 carrots, sliced

375 g/12 oz cooked chick peas (see pages 78–79)

chopped coriander and coriander sprigs, to garnish

couscous (see page 66), to serve

1 Heat the oil in a saucepan. Add the onion, garlic, chilli and ginger and cook over a medium heat, stirring frequently, until the onion has softened and is lightly browned. Add the cumin, ground coriander and allspice and stir for 1 minute, then add the chicken. Pour in the stock and heat to simmering point. Cover and simmer over a low heat for 30 minutes.

2 Add the red pepper, courgette and carrots. Cover and continue to simmer for 30 minutes, until the vegetables are tender.

3 Add the chick peas to the pan and simmer, uncovered, for 5 minutes.

4 Make a bed of couscous on a large, warmed serving dish. Put the chicken in the centre. Scoop the vegetables from the casserole using a slotted spoon and add to the chicken. Pour the cooking juices over the chicken and couscous. Scatter over the chopped coriander, garnish with coriander sprigs and serve the dish immediately.

Desserts
and
Puddings

How to Make Hot Puddings

Creamed Sponge Pudding Mixes

A creamed sponge mixture is a great standby since it can be transformed by adding simple flavouring ingredients. It is equally good baked, steamed or cooked in the microwave.

Basic Sponge Pudding Mix

Serves: **4**

Preparation time: 10 minutes

Cooking time: 5 minutes–2 hours (depending on method)

75 g/3 oz butter or block margarine
75 g/3 oz caster sugar or soft brown sugar
1 egg
150 g/5 oz self-raising flour
a little milk

1 Butter a 900 ml/1½ pint ovenproof dish or pudding basin.

2 Cream together the butter or margarine and sugar until light and fluffy. Add the egg and beat well.

3 Fold in the flour and add just enough milk to make a dropping consistency. Spoon the mixture into the prepared dish and spread it out evenly.

To Bake: Bake for 30–35 minutes in a preheated oven at 180°C/350°F/Gas Mark 4.

To Steam: Cover with greased greaseproof paper and foil, folding the foil firmly around the rim of the dish or basin to prevent moisture from entering. Steam for 1½–2 hours.

To Microwave: Cover with a piece of greaseproof paper and cook on high (100% power) for 5–6 minutes. Stand for 1 minute before serving.

VARIATIONS

Jam or Syrup Sponge

Place 3 tablespoons jam or syrup in the base of the dish before adding the mixture.

Chocolate Chip and Walnut Pudding

Stir in 25 g/1 oz chocolate chips and 2 tablespoons chopped walnuts with the milk.

Coconut and Cherry Pudding

Stir in 2 tablespoons desiccated coconut and 50 g/2 oz chopped glacé cherries before adding the milk.

Orange or Lemon Pudding

Stir in the finely grated rind of 1 orange or lemon with the flour and orange or lemon juice instead of milk. For steamed puddings, arrange slices of citrus fruit in the bottom of the basin before adding the mixture.

Tips for Perfect Steamed Puddings

A properly cooked steamed pudding should be light, fluffy and moist, never soggy. Just follow these simple rules.

1 Before you start, half-fill the base of a steamer or saucepan with water and put it on to boil. If you do not have a steamer, use a large saucepan and pour in enough water to come just half-way up the outside of the basin in which the pudding is to be cooked.

2 Grease the basin well, then insert a small circle of greaseproof paper in the bottom of the basin to ensure that the pudding turns out easily.

3 Fill the basin no more than two-thirds full, to allow for the mixture to rise.

4 To cover the basin, grease a large piece of greaseproof paper and make a pleat across the centre to allow room for the paper to expand when the pudding rises. Cut and pleat a piece of foil. Cover the basin first with the paper, then with the foil, sealing the edges thoroughly on to the rim to prevent steam entering and making the pudding soggy.

5 The water should be boiling by the time the mixture is ready. Once the pudding is in the steamer, keep the water at a constant, gentle boil. If it goes off the boil, even briefly, the pudding may be soggy. Have a kettle of boiling water ready to top up the water as necessary, to prevent the pan boiling dry and burning.

Tips for Fail-safe Soufflés

The base mixture for a hot, sweet soufflé (whether it is a sauce or fruit purée) should be the consistency of softly whipped cream. If the mixture is too stiff, it will be difficult to fold in the egg whites; if it is too soft, the mixture will not hold enough air to make a light soufflé.

The whisked egg whites provide about half the volume of the soufflé, so it is important to

whisk them until they are stiff enough to hold soft peaks, but not dry. Fold in the whites lightly and evenly, avoiding knocking out the air and leaving no white clumps.

Use a greased, straight-sided dish so that the mixture rises up the sides evenly. For a 'top-hat' effect, use a sharp knife to cut through the mixture just inside the edge of the dish just before cooking.

Quick and Easy Toppings for Fruit

Use these simple toppings to turn plain stewed fruit into a substantial hot pudding.

Cobbler

Any sweet scone mixture can be used to make a cobbler topping. Roll out the dough to about 1 cm/½ inch thick, then use a biscuit cutter to stamp out rounds or fancy shapes. Arrange these overlapping slightly on top of the fruit in

an ovenproof dish. Brush with milk and bake in a preheated oven at 200°C/400°F/Gas Mark 6 for 10–15 minutes or until the scones (cobblers) are well-risen, firm and golden brown.

Spiced Bread

Dice 3 slices wholemeal bread (crusts removed). Melt about 25 g/1 oz butter in a saucepan and stir in the bread to coat the pieces evenly. Scatter over the fruit, sprinkle lightly with demerara sugar and bake in a preheated oven at 200°C/400°F/Gas Mark 6 for 15–20 minutes, until golden brown and crisp.

Filo Chiffon

Brush 3 sheets of filo pastry with melted butter and scrunch them over the fruit in an ovenproof dish. Bake in a preheated oven at 200°C/400°F/Gas Mark 6 for 10–15 minutes until golden and crisp. Sprinkle the pudding with icing sugar before serving hot, warm or cold (but not chilled).

Bread and Butter Pudding

This simple, inexpensive pudding is as light as air and tastes quite sublime. You can serve it with cream or stewed fruit, if liked.

Serves: **4**

Preparation time: 15 minutes, plus standing

Cooking time: 30–40 minutes

Oven temperature: 180°C/350°F/Gas Mark 4

50 g/2 oz unsalted butter
4 thin slices day-old white bread
50 g/2 oz sultanas
25 g/1 oz mixed peel (optional)
grated rind of 1 lemon
300 ml/½ pint single cream and 300 ml/½ pint milk or 600 ml/1 pint milk
2 eggs
2 egg yolks
25 g/1 oz sugar
½ teaspoon grated nutmeg
1–2 tablespoons jelly marmalade, heated

1 Butter the slices of bread and cut each into 4 triangles. Place a layer of bread in the base of a buttered 1 litre/1¾ pint pie dish. Sprinkle the sultanas, mixed peel and grated lemon rind over the top and cover with the remaining bread triangles.

2 Beat the cream, if using, with the milk, eggs, egg yolks and sugar. Strain the mixture over the bread. Set aside to stand for 30 minutes.

3 Grate a little nutmeg over the surface and bake in a preheated oven, 180°C/350°F/Gas Mark 4, for 30–40 minutes.

4 When the pudding is cooked, remove it from the oven and brush the hot marmalade over the top. Serve hot.

VARIATION • You can glaze the top of the pudding with warmed apricot jam instead of marmalade.

Christmas Pudding with Brandy Butter

Nothing beats a home-made pudding at Christmastime. It is not difficult to make, but is time-consuming and quite hard work. Make the most of the old tradition of everyone in the family stirring the pudding three times for a wish to minimise the strain on your own wrists!

Serves: **6**

Preparation time: 30–40 minutes

Cooking time: 6 hours

125 g/4 oz self-raising flour
125 g/4 oz fresh breadcrumbs
125 g/4 oz shredded suet
375 g/12 oz mixed dried fruit (apricots, raisins, sultanas, currants, dates, prunes)
50 g/2 oz mixed peel, chopped
50 g/2 oz blanched almonds, chopped
125 g/4 oz dark brown sugar
grated rind and juice of 1 lemon
grated rind and juice of 1 orange
½ teaspoon ground mixed spice
¼ teaspoon grated nutmeg
pinch of salt
3 eggs, beaten
about 150 ml/¼ pint dark brown ale or stout

1 Put all the ingredients into a mixing bowl and mix thoroughly. The mixture should have a soft dropping consistency – add a little more ale or stout if necessary. Spoon the mixture into a greased 1.2 litre/2 pint pudding basin. Cover with pleated greased greaseproof paper and foil and tie securely (see page 194–5).

2 Put the basin in a saucepan and add sufficient boiling water to come halfway up the side of the basin. Cover tightly and steam the pudding for up to 6 hours (see pages 194–195). Check the level of the water at frequent intervals and top up with more boiling water whenever necessary.

3 Either serve the pudding straight away, with the brandy butter, or store in a cool place for up to one year.

4 To reheat, steam, as before, for a further 2 hours. To serve, remove the covering and run a round-bladed knife around the inside of the basin. Place a serving plate on top and invert the pudding.

BRANDY BUTTER
Serves: **6**

Preparation time: 10 minutes

150 g/5 oz unsalted butter
150 g/5 oz caster sugar
3–4 tablespoons brandy

Cream the butter until soft, then gradually add the sugar and brandy, beating thoroughly with each addition. Pile into a serving dish. Chill until firm.

FOOD FACT • For a traditional flamed pudding, gently heat 2 tablespoons brandy in a saucepan until warm. Pour the brandy over the pudding, stand back and ignite. Wait until the flames have died down before cutting and serving with the brandy butter.

Making Cold Desserts

Ice Creams and Sorbets

Flavouring Iced Mixtures

When making mixtures for sorbets or ice creams, remember that freezing tends to dull the sweetness and flavour, so the mixture should taste slightly too sweet for best results when frozen. This also applies to additional flavourings, such as vanilla, which can be used in greater quantity than usual.

Getting the Texture Right

The best texture for sorbets and ice creams is obtained by continuous whisking, which breaks down ice crystals and creates a satin-smooth result. An electric ice cream maker does the whisking while the mixture freezes,

so if you make ices often this might be a worthwhile investment.

If you do not have an ice cream maker, turn the unfrozen mixture into a freezerproof container to a depth of about 5 cm/2 inches and freeze it for about 1 hour or until the edge of the mixture is becoming slushy. Remove from the freezer and whisk hard with an electric hand whisk or turn the mixture into a food processor and process until smooth. Return the mixture to the container and freeze again. Repeat this process a further 2–3 times, at intervals of about 1 hour.

Once frozen, leave the ice in the freezer for at least 24 hours for the flavour to mature. Most ices benefit from being transferred to the refrigerator for about 20 minutes before serving, making them easier to scoop or slice and allowing their flavours to develop.

Making Caramel

Slowly melt 175 g/6 oz caster or granulated sugar in a heavy-based saucepan over a low heat. Once melted, increase the heat to high and cook the sugar until it turns to a rich, brown caramel. Immediately remove from the heat and pour out of the pan as required.

Coating with Caramel

To coat dishes with caramel, for example before adding custard for crème caramel, first rinse the dish in hot water. This prevents the caramel from setting too quickly or cracking a cold dish. Holding the dish with a cloth, quickly pour in the hot, liquid caramel. Tilt and swirl the dish as you pour in the caramel to coat the base and sides evenly.

Making Caramel Decorations

Lightly oil a baking sheet before making the caramel. Drizzle the caramel in zig-zag shapes

over the baking sheet. Leave them to set, then carefully lift off the shapes with a palette knife and use as decoration for desserts. Alternatively, pour the caramel in a single layer on to the sheet and leave to set. Then break the hard caramel into rough, pointed shards.

Making Brûlée Toppings

Grilling

To top Crème Brûlée with caramel, chill the custard bases well, then sprinkle the tops with a thick, even layer of caster or demerara sugar. Preheat a grill to very hot and place the dishes as close as possible to the heat to melt and caramelise the sugar. Leave to set hard.

Blowtorch

A small blowtorch is the ideal tool for making a perfect brûlée topping, since you can control the browning easily. Sprinkle the dishes with sugar as above and keep the blowtorch moving quickly over the surface until the sugar melts and caramelises. Leave until set hard.

1 To turn out a set jelly or moulded dessert, first wet the serving plate lightly with cold water. This will allow you to move the dessert slightly if it is not exactly in the middle. Run the tip of a knife around the edge of the dessert.
2 Dip the base of the mould briefly in a bowl of hot water. Place the plate on top, then quickly invert both plate and mould, giving a sharp shake to turn out the set mixture on to the plate. If the mixture does not turn out, try holding a hot, wet cloth over the mould briefly.

Using Cream for Desserts

Cream is classified by its fat content, which determines its texture and the use for which it is best suited. Single cream has a pouring consistency: it will not whip or become light or thick. Soured cream, crème fraîche and clotted cream cannot be whipped, but are used for spooning or pouring.

Only whipping cream and double cream are suitable for whipping. Whipping cream has a lower fat content than double cream: it takes slightly longer to whip and gives a lighter result. Double cream whips quickly, but take care not to overwhip it. When overwhipped it looks very firm, buttery and slightly grainy in texture.

How to Whip Cream

Use a clean, dry bowl and, ideally, a balloon whisk. A hand-held electric whisk is fine used on low speed, but take care not to overwhip cream. Cream whips more successfully when chilled first, giving greater volume. Whip the cream slowly, pausing occasionally to check the consistency. Stop as soon as it is thick enough to hold its shape. The heat of your hand holding a piping bag or the action of spreading or stirring will cause the cream to stiffen further.

Dissolving Powdered Gelatine

Method 1

When dissolving gelatine in a small quantity of liquid before adding it to a mixture which is to be set, sprinkle the powder over the cold liquid (usually at least 3 tablespoons water) in a small bowl. Do not stir, but leave to stand until the gelatine has absorbed the water and looks spongy. Then stand the bowl in a saucepan of hot water and stir occasionally until it has dissolved completely.

Method 2

When dissolving gelatine in a large quantity of liquid, always sprinkle the gelatine on to the liquid, not the other way round. Use hot liquid, and stir thoroughly to dissolve the crystals. If the gelatine does not completely dissolve (you should be able to see if there are any crystals left undissolved), stand the jug or bowl in a pan of hot water over a low heat. Leave until the gelatine has completely dissolved, but never allow the gelatine to boil.

Some fresh fruit, such as pineapple, papaya and kiwifruit, contain an enzyme that will prevent gelatine from setting. Cooking the fruit for just a few minutes will kill the enzyme and eliminate the problem.

Never add dissolved gelatine to a very cold mixture since it will set into ribbons before you have time to mix it in properly. Ideally, the two should be at a similar temperature. Work quickly so that the ingredients are evenly mixed, then chill until set.

Chocolate and Orange Bombe

Home-made ice cream is a revelation to the taste buds. Serve this spectacular bombe on a special occasion and you will be guaranteed a success.

Serves: **8**

Preparation time: 15–20 minutes, plus freezing

Cooking time: 5 minutes

ORANGE ICE CREAM
finely grated rind and juice of 2 oranges
3 eggs, separated
150 g/5 oz caster sugar
300 ml/½ pint double cream, lightly whipped
CHOCOLATE FILLING
125 g/4 oz plain chocolate, chopped
4 tablespoons single cream
TO DECORATE
Chocolate Leaves (see page 243)
fine strips of orange rind

1 First make the orange ice cream. Put the orange rind, egg yolks and half the sugar in a bowl. Whisk with an electric mixer until thick. In a separate bowl, whisk the egg whites until stiff (see pages 22–23), then gradually whisk in the remaining sugar.

2 Whisk the orange juice into the whipped cream. Fold into the egg mixture, then fold into the egg white mixture. Turn into a rigid freezerproof container, cover, seal and freeze until firm.

3 Place the chocolate and cream in a small pan and heat gently, stirring constantly, until the chocolate has melted. Remove the pan from the heat and set aside to cool.

4 Line the sides of a chilled 1.5 litre/2½ pint bombe mould or freezerproof basin thickly with the orange ice cream. Fill the centre with the chocolate filling and cover with any remaining ice cream. Put on the lid of the bombe mould or cover the basin with foil and freeze for 4 hours.

5 Dip the mould or basin into cold water and turn the bombe out onto a chilled serving dish, decorate with chocolate leaves and strips of orange rind and serve.

Apricot and Orange Mousse

Serves: **4–6**

Preparation time: 30 minutes, plus chilling and soaking

Cooking time: 40 minutes

250 g/8 oz dried apricots
600 ml/1 pint boiling water
grated rind of 1 orange
juice of 2 oranges
15 g/½ oz powered gelatine
50–75 g/2–3 oz caster sugar, to taste
150 ml/¼ pint double cream, lightly whipped
2 egg whites
langue de chat biscuits, to serve (optional)
TO DECORATE
150 ml/¼ pint double cream, whipped
rind of ½ orange, cut into julienne strips and
    blanched for 5 minutes

1 Put the apricots into a saucepan, pour over the boiling water, cover and set aside to soak for 2 hours.

2 Bring the apricots and soaking water to the boil over a low heat, then add the grated orange rind. Cover and simmer very gently, stirring occasionally, for 40 minutes, until the apricots are very soft. Remove the pan from the heat. Stir in half the orange juice.

3 Put the gelatine into a bowl, pour over the remaining orange juice and set aside to soak for 5 minutes. Heat gently until dissolved (see page 201).

4 Stir sugar to taste into the apricots, then rub the fruit and juice through a nylon sieve set over a bowl. Stir the dissolved gelatine into the apricot purée, then set aside until cool and just beginning to thicken.

5 Fold the lightly whipped cream into the purée. Whisk the egg whites until they are holding their shape and fold into the mixture (see pages 22–23).

6 Spoon into a serving bowl or dish and refrigerate for 1½–2 hours until set.

7 Spoon a layer of whipped cream on to the mousse and scatter the orange julienne in the centre. Serve chilled with langue de chat biscuits, if liked.

Nectarine Brûlée

Serve this pretty dessert with special biscuits, such as brandy snaps, langues du chat or amaretti.

Serves: **6**

Preparation time: 10 minutes

Cooking time: 10–15 minutes

500 g/1 lb nectarines, pitted and sliced
4 tablespoons orange liqueur, plus extra to flavour fruit
350 ml/12 fl oz soured cream
pinch of grated nutmeg
1 teaspoon vanilla essence
125 g/4 oz light brown sugar

1 Put the nectarines in a saucepan and add enough water to cover. Poach over a low heat for 5–10 minutes, or until tender. Drain and divide between 6 individual ramekins. Stir in a little orange liqueur.

2 Beat together the soured cream, nutmeg, vanilla and remaining orange liqueur until blended. Spoon over the nectarine slices, then scatter the brown sugar over the top in a thick layer. Grill under a preheated hot grill until the sugar caramelises.

VARIATIONS • Use fresh apricots, peaches or pineapple instead of nectarines. Double cream may be used instead of soured cream. The nutmeg may be replaced by cinnamon, and the orange liqueur by rum.

Bread and Yeast

Types of Flour and Yeast

Flour

There is now a huge choice of flours available, all of which can be used for bread and yeast baking, but all with individual characteristics that produce very different results.

Plain Flour

Plain flour is known as a 'soft' flour because it has a low gluten content. Gluten becomes tough and elastic when mixed with liquid and kneaded or beaten. It makes a dough stretch and hold air.

Strong Flour

Strong flour has a high gluten content. It absorbs moisture and becomes springy and elastic when mixed to a dough. This gives the dough greater capacity for expansion. Most bread and yeast recipes use strong flour. Although ordinary plain flour can be used, it gives a close-textured, more crumbly loaf.

Wholemeal Flour

This contains 100% of the wholemeal grain. It is high in fibre and has a distinctive flavour and nutty texture. Bread made with this flour tends to be heavy and close-textured. Use a mixture of half wholemeal and half white flour to counteract this.

Brown Flour

This contains about 85% of the wheat grain, with some germ and bran removed. It can be used to make a high-fibre, lighter loaf.

White Flour

This usually contains 75% of the wheat grain, with most of the bran and wheatgerm removed during milling.

Wheatgerm Flour

This is white or brown flour with at least 10% added wheatgerm.

Stoneground Flour

This takes its name from the milling process of grinding between huge granite stones, which heats the grain and gives it a slightly roasted, nutty flavour.

Malted Wheatgrain – Granary or Wheatberry Flour

These are brown or wholemeal flours that have added malted wheat grains or flakes, giving the flour a nutty texture and distinctive malted flavour.

Rye Flour

This is often used for bread, particularly the traditional German pumpernickel, but because it is low in gluten, it produces a heavy, close-textured loaf. To make a lighter loaf, mix it in about equal quantities with strong white or brown flour.

Spelt Flour

Spelt is an ancient strain of wheat with a high gluten content and unique, nutty, wheat-like flavour. This flour can be used in any recipe calling for wholemeal flour.

Organic Flour

This is flour milled from grain grown without the use of artificial fertilisers or pesticides on organic farms.

Other Flours

Various other flours or grains, such as cornmeal, oatmeal, barley, buckwheat or millet, can be used for making breads. To obtain a good texture, they are best mixed with strong wheat flour. Coarse cornmeal, or polenta, gives bread a lovely crunchy crust if you sprinkle it over the surface of a greased tin or baking sheet before adding the dough. Sprinkle crushed, flaked or rolled grains over loaves or rolls after glazing for an attractive, nutty topping.

Yeast

All types of yeast have the same rising properties and are interchangeable in most recipes, with slight variations in the method. The choice of yeast is a matter of convenience and personal preference.

Fresh Yeast

For best results, fresh yeast should be very fresh: ideally, buy it in small quantities just as you need it, but it can be wrapped in clingfilm and stored for 2–3 weeks in the refrigerator. It should be pale beige in colour and moist but slightly crumbly in texture, with a slight winey smell. It should not have dried or discoloured patches. Fresh yeast can be frozen: wrap 25 g/1 oz portions individually in clingfilm, pack them in a freezer bag and store for up to 3 months. They thaw quickly ready for use. 25 g/1 oz fresh yeast is usually enough to rise 1.5 kg/3 lb flour, but this may vary depending on the other ingredients in the recipe.

Dried Yeast

More convenient and easier to buy than fresh yeast, this will keep in an airtight container for about 6 months. The tiny dry granules are reconstituted in liquid with a little sugar to activate them – this takes about 15 minutes. Be sure to buy baker's yeast, not brewer's yeast, which is not suitable for yeast cookery. Dried yeast is concentrated, so you will need about half the quantity of fresh yeast. It is easier to measure dried yeast in spoonfuls: if a recipe calls for 25 g/1 oz fresh yeast, use 1 tablespoon dried yeast.

Fast-action and Easy-blend Yeasts

These are dried yeasts. The fine granules should be added straight to the flour and are quickly activated. These yeasts need only 1 rising and proving, instead of the usual 2 stages. A 15 g/½ oz sachet is usually enough to rise 750 g/1½ lb strong white flour, but more may be needed for enriched doughs.

How to Make Bread Doughs

Dissolving Yeast

Crumble fresh yeast into measured, hand-hot liquid (1 part boiling to 2 parts cold water) and stir lightly with a fork to dissolve the yeast. Leave to soak for 2–5 minutes before adding the liquid to the dry ingredients.

To use dried yeast, add about 1 teaspoon caster sugar to the measured hand-hot liquid, then sprinkle the yeast granules over, stirring lightly with a fork to separate the granules. Before adding it to the dry ingredients, leave the mixture undisturbed in a warm place for about 15 minutes, until it froths up.

Add easy-blend yeast to the flour or dry ingredients and mix well before adding liquid.

Kneading

Kneading is essential to develop the gluten and strengthen the dough, giving an even rise and light texture. You can do this by hand, with a dough hook on a food mixer or using the dough blade for a food processor. Follow the manufacturer's instructions for best results.

To knead by hand, turn out the dough on to a lightly floured work surface. Fold the dough towards you, then use the heel of your hand to push it down and away from you. Give the dough a quarter turn and repeat the folding and pushing movement. Continue in this way for 5–10 minutes, or until the dough feels smooth, elastic and no longer sticky.

Quick White Bread

Makes: **1 large loaf or 12 rolls**
Preparation time: 20 minutes, plus rising
Cooking time: 15–35 minutes

750 g/1¼ lb strong white flour
2 teaspoons salt
1 sachet fast-action easy-blend dried yeast
2 tablespoons vegetable oil or melted butter
450 ml/¾ pint hand-hot water
milk to glaze

1 Grease a baking sheet or 1 kg/2 1b loaf tin. Mix the flour, salt and yeast in a large bowl and make a well in the centre. Pour in the oil or butter and water, then mix quickly to bring all the ingredients together into a rough ball.
2 Turn out on to a floured surface and knead until smooth. Shape into a loaf or rolls and put in the prepared tin or on the baking sheet.
3 Cover with lightly oiled polythene or a dampened tea towel and leave in a warm place for 45–60 minutes, until the dough has doubled in size and is springy to the touch. Rolls will rise more quickly than a large loaf.
4 Brush the bread with milk, then bake in a preheated oven at 220°C/425°F/Gas Mark 7 until golden brown. Allow 15–18 minutes for rolls or 30–35 minutes for a large loaf.
5 To test if the bread is cooked, turn it out of the tin, or lift from the baking sheet, and tap it underneath with your knuckles. When cooked, it should sound hollow. Cool on a wire rack.

Flavouring the Basic Loaf

Add any of the following dry ingredients after kneading but before shaping the dough. Knead them in briefly until evenly distributed.

Tomato and Olive

Use olive oil instead of the vegetable oil or butter. Add 75 g/3 oz sun-dried tomatoes, chopped, and 75 g/3 oz pitted black or green olives, halved.

Walnut and Thyme

Use walnut oil instead of the vegetable oil or butter. Add 50 g/2 oz walnuts, chopped, and 2 tablespoons chopped fresh thyme.

Pine Nut and Pesto

Replace the oil with Pesto alla Genovese (see page 37) and add 50 g/2 oz pine nuts.

Onion and Rosemary

Add 1 red onion, thinly sliced, and 1 tablespoon chopped fresh rosemary. Sprinkle the shaped bread with grated cheese, such as Parmesan or Cheddar, before baking.

Shaping Loaves or Rolls

Plait

Divide the dough into three equal pieces and shape each into a long, thin sausage. Pinch the three strands together at one end and plait loosely down the length. Pinch the ends together to hold in place.

Knot

Roll out the dough to a long sausage, then tie loosely into a knot.

Cottage

Cut off about a third of the dough and shape both pieces into rounds. Put the small round on top of the larger round and press a wooden spoon handle down through the middle of both rounds.

Glorious Glazes

Apply to the risen dough just before baking.

Soft Crust

Brush with milk or oil and dust with flour.

Crisp Crust

Brush with 1 teaspoon salt dissolved in 1 tablespoon water.

Shiny Crust

Beat 1 egg with a pinch of salt and brush over.

Glazing Cooked Breads

Brush baked rolls or loaves with maple syrup or warmed clear honey as soon as they come out of the oven for a glossy, sweet glaze.

Focaccia

This rustic Italian bread is delicious served with minestrone, pasta, risotto or simply with cheese.

Serves: **4**

Preparation time: 20 minutes, plus rising

Cooking time: 15–25 minutes

Oven temperature: 200°C/400°F/Gas Mark 6

10 g/⅓ oz fresh yeast or 2 teaspoons dried yeast
about 300 ml/½ pint warm milk
500 g/1 lb unbleached strong white flour, plus extra for dusting
pinch of salt
3–5 tablespoons virgin olive oil, plus extra for brushing
coarse sea salt
rosemary leaves (optional)

1 Blend or dissolve the yeast with the milk and leave until frothy (see page 212). Sift the flour and salt into a large warmed bowl and make a well in the centre. Slowly pour in the yeast liquid and oil, stirring the dry ingredients into the liquid to make a smooth, soft but not wet dough. Add a little more milk if necessary. Turn on to a floured surface and knead until smooth and elastic. Place the dough in a clean bowl, cover and set aside at room temperature until doubled in bulk.

2 Flour a baking sheet. Tip the dough on to a floured surface and knead for 2–3 minutes. Roll the dough into a large circle about 5–10 mm/¼–½ inch thick – the thicker it is, the chewier the bread. Carefully transfer the dough to the baking sheet, keeping the circular shape. Brush with olive oil, sprinkle with coarse salt and scatter over a few rosemary leaves, if liked. With the end of a wooden spoon or a clean finger, make deep indentations over the surface of the dough. Spray with water and set aside until doubled in bulk. Meanwhile, put a baking tin in the oven to heat for 20 minutes.

3 Put the loaf in the oven and fill the baking tin with hot water. Immediately close the oven door and bake the loaf in the preheated oven, 200°C/400°F/Gas Mark 6, for 15–20 minutes if 5 mm/¼ inch thick, 20–25 minutes if slightly thicker, until golden and the underneath sounds hollow when tapped. Serve warm.

VARIATION • To make focaccia with herbs, knead 10–12 torn sage leaves or 2 teaspoons rosemary leaves into the dough at the second kneading. Shape and set aside to rise as above. Brush with an extra tablespoon of olive oil before baking.

Dresden Christmas Stollen

At Christmas, most German families serve this delicious fruit bread, which is rich and decorated with colourful candied fruits for the occasion. This stollen tastes best when eaten fresh. However, if well wrapped in aluminium foil, it will keep for 3–4 days and when dry can be sliced and toasted.

Serves: **8–10**

Preparation time: 45 minutes, plus soaking and rising

Cooking time: 1 hour

Oven temperature: 230°C/450°F/Gas Mark 8, then 200°C/400°F/Gas Mark 6

75 g/3 oz sultanas
75 g/3 oz raisins
25 g/1 oz glacé cherries, halved
25 g/1 oz flaked almonds, toasted
50 g/2 oz candied lemon peel, chopped
grated rind of 1 lemon
25 ml/1 fl oz rum or brandy
500 g/1 lb plain flour
pinch of salt
¼ teaspoon ground mace or grated nutmeg
25 g/1 oz dried yeast
50 ml/2 fl oz lukewarm milk
125 ml/4 fl oz lukewarm water
25 g/1 oz caster sugar
125 g/4 oz butter, softened, plus extra for greasing
about 40 g/1½ oz butter, melted
GLAZE
4 tablespoons sugar
4 tablespoons boiling water
TO DECORATE
mixed candied fruits
citrus peel
glacé cherries

1 Put the fruit, nuts, peel and grated lemon rind in a bowl and pour the rum or brandy over them. Set aside to soak, preferably overnight, until the liquid is absorbed.

2 Sift the flour, salt and spice into a warmed mixing bowl. Mix the yeast with the warm milk and water and a teaspoon of the sugar, sprinkle with flour and set aside in a warm place (see page 212).

3 Stir the yeast mixture into the flour with the remaining sugar and mix into a dough. Beat in the softened butter. Turn the dough on to a floured board and knead for 10 minutes, until smooth and elastic.

4 Put the dough into a clean bowl, cover and set aside in a warm place for 30 minutes, or until doubled in size.

5 Punch the dough to knock it back, and work in the fruit, one-third at a time. Do this quickly or the dough will discolour. Shape into an oval. Roll out to about 2.5 cm/1 inch thick. Make a dent lengthways with the rolling pin, slightly off-centre. Fold the narrower side over on to the wide side and press down. Place the stollen on a greased baking sheet, cover and set aside in a warm place for about 20 minutes, or until puffy.

6 Brush the stollen with melted butter and bake in a preheated oven, 230°C/450°F/Gas Mark 8, for 30 minutes. Reduce the heat to 200°C/400°F/Gas Mark 6 and continue baking for a further 20–30 minutes. When cooked, a skewer inserted into it should come out clean.

5 Dissolve the sugar in the water for the glaze. While the stollen is still hot, brush with sugar glaze. When decorating for Christmas, arrange mixed candied fruit on top of the stollen and brush again with the sugar glaze.

Classic Tomato Pizza

Serves: **4**

Preparation time: 18–20 minutes

Cooking time: 10 minutes

Oven temperature: 230°C/450°F/Gas Mark 8

3 tablespoons olive oil
2 red onions, sliced finely
2 garlic cloves, crushed and chopped
2 x 400 g/13 oz cans chopped tomatoes
1 teaspoon red wine vinegar
sugar, to taste
8 anchovy fillets, cut in to thin lengths
2 tablespoons pitted black olives
1 tablespoon capers
250 g/8 oz mozzarella cheese, sliced
salt and pepper
PIZZA BASE
250 g/8 oz self raising flour
1 teaspoon salt
150 ml/¼ pint warm water

1 First make the pizza base. Sift the flour and salt into a large bowl. Gradually add the water and mix to form a soft dough. When it has bound together, mix the dough with your hands into a ball. Turn the dough out on a lightly floured surface and knead until smooth and soft.

2 Divide the dough into 4 and, with your hands and a rolling pin, flatten it as thinly as possible. The pizza rounds do not have to be exact circles, since that is one of the charms of making your own pizzas. Make the pizzas just a bit smaller than your serving plates.

3 To make the topping, heat the oil in a large saucepan. Add the onion and garlic and fry over a medium heat, stirring frequently, for 3 minutes. Add the tomatoes, vinegar and sugar and season to taste with salt and pepper. Increase the heat and simmer the mixture until it has reduced by half to make a thick and rich tomato sauce.

4 Place the pizza bases on warmed baking sheets, spoon over the sauce and spread to the edge with the back of the spoon.

5 Arrange the anchovies on the pizzas, sprinkle with the olives and capers and finally add the mozzarella. Bake the pizzas in a preheated oven, 230°C/450°F/Gas Mark 8, for 10 minutes until golden and sizzling.

Pastry

How to Make Pastry

Choice of Flour

Plain white flour is the best choice for most pastries, giving a light, crisp pastry. Self-raising flour gives a softer sponge-like texture, recommended for suet crust which will be heavy without a raising agent. Wholemeal flour, or a mixture of half wholemeal and half white, can be used for shortcrust pastry, but this gives a heavy, crumbly dough which can be difficult to handle. Puff, flaky or rough puff pastries are usually made with strong plain flour, since this gives the dough more elasticity and strength.

Choice of Fats

The type of fat affects the texture as well as the flavour of the pastry.

Butter, preferably unsalted, gives the best colour and flavour, but used on its own it can be rich and oily. Margarine is good for colour, but the flavour is less good and depends very much on quality. Soft margarine should only be used for fork-mix, all-in-one pastry. Lard gives a good short, crumbly texture, but it lacks flavour and colour when used on its own. If you prefer not to use lard, a good-quality white vegetable fat can be used instead.

The best shortcrust pastry is made using equal quantities of butter or margarine with lard or white vegetable fat.

Secrets of Successful Pastry

Measure the right proportions of fat to flour, according to the type of pastry. For shortcrust pastry, use double the weight of flour to fat. Richer short pastries use a higher proportion of fat to flour.

Except with choux pastry, keep everything, including your hands, as cool as possible.

When rubbing in fats, use only the very tips of your fingers to keep the mixture cool. Lift the fingers high, letting the crumbs run through them back into the bowl. Alternatively, use a food processor to rub in the fat evenly and pulse the power to make sure that the pastry is not overmixed. Light handling also applies when rolling out and shaping pastry – overhandling makes heavy pastry.

Do not add the full amount of liquid all at once. Flours vary in absorbency and too much liquid can make the pastry heavy.

With the exception of choux and suet crust, pastry benefits from resting for about 20–30 minutes before baking. This reduces shrinkage during cooking and is particularly important for pastries that are handled a great deal during preparation, such as puff or rough puff. Wrap the pastry in clingfilm to prevent it from drying out and place in the refrigerator.

It is vital to preheat the oven thoroughly, particularly for pastries with a high fat content which should be cooked at a high temperature for light, crisp resuls.

How Much Pastry?

When a recipe gives a guide to the quantity of shortcrust pastry required, the weight usually refers to the amount of flour. For example, if the recipe requires 200 g/7 oz shortcrust pastry, make the dough from 200 g/7 oz flour, plus fat and other ingredients in proportion. Using this guide, you can work out approximately how much pastry to make for different sizes of flan tins.

Flan Tin Diameter	Pastry Quantity
18 cm/7 inch	125 g/4 oz
20 cm/8 inch	175 g/6 oz
23 cm/9 inch	200 g/7 oz
25 cm/10 inch	250 g/8 oz
4 x10 cm/4 inch individual tins	150 g/5 oz

How to Shape and Use Pastry

Rolling Out

Dust a cool worksurface and a rolling pin lightly with flour. Roll lightly and evenly in one direction, always away from you, turning the pastry a quarter turn occasionally. Try to keep the pastry even in shape and thickness. Avoid stretching the pastry, since this causes it to shrink during cooking. Depending on the recipe, shortcrust pastry is usually rolled to about 3 mm/⅛ inch thick; puff pastry can be rolled slightly thicker, to about 5 mm/¼ inch.

Covering a Pie Dish

Single-crust Pie

1 Roll out the pastry to about 5 cm/2 inches larger than the dish (use the inverted dish as a guide).

2 Cut off a 2.5 cm/1 inch wide strip around the edge. Moisten the rim of the dish with water and press the pastry strip on to it.

3 Add the pie filling, piling it slightly towards the centre to give the top crust a good shape. Brush the pastry rim with a little water.

4 Carefully lift the pastry by rolling it loosely over the rolling pin and place it over the pie. Then unroll the pastry over the pie and press the edges together to seal in the filling.

5 Use a sharp knife to trim off excess pastry from the edge, cutting from the underneath at an angle away from the pie. Cut a steam vent in the centre with the point of the knife.

Double-crust Pie

These are made with shortcrust pastry, since rich, puff or flaky pastries do not cook well underneath filling. It is best if the filling is cold when added to the pastry base, because hot fillings tend to melt the pastry.

1 Divide the pastry into 2 separate portions, one slightly larger than the other. Use the larger piece for the base of the pie. Measure the depth of the dish and add this to the diameter, then roll out the pastry to about 1.5 cm/¾ inch larger.

2 Lift the pastry over the rolling pin and lower it gently into the dish. Ease it into the sides, without stretching, and press it against the rim.

3 Use the remaining pastry to make a single crust (see left).

Finishing Pie Edges

Flaking the Edge or Knocking Up

This helps to seal the pastry neatly, preventing fillings from leaking out. Hold one finger lightly against the top of the pastry rim, then press the blade of a knife horizontally into the cut pastry edge, making a series of shallow cuts. Do this all around the edge.

Scalloped Edge

This is a decorative finish to make a pie crust look professional, but it also helps to seal the edge more firmly.

Place the knife blade at a vertical angle against the pastry edge and press your fingertip next to it on the rim. Make a vertical cut, pulling slightly upwards, to create a scallop. Continue around the edge at intervals of about 1.5 cm/¾ inch all around the pie.

Crimping the Edge

This is a quick and simple alternative to flaking and scalloping pastry edges. Push the finger of one hand into the top of the pastry rim. At the same time, pinch the outer edge with the finger and thumb of the other hand, pinching

the pastry to a point. Continue all around the edge of the pie.

Lining a Flan Tin

Place the flan ring or tin on a baking sheet. Roll out the pastry to about 5 cm/2 inches larger all round than the diameter of the ring or tin. Roll the pastry loosely around the rolling pin and lift it over the tin, then carefully unroll it into the tin.

Gently ease the pastry into the tin, pressing it into the flutes with your finger and taking care not to stretch it or leave air gaps underneath. Turn any surplus pastry outwards from the rim, then roll the rolling pin straight over the top so that the surplus pastry is cut and falls away, to leave a neat edge.

Baking Pastry Blind

This is a method of part-baking the pastry in the tin before adding filling. The pastry is weighted down to prevent it from bubbling up or falling down around the side.

Line the flan tin as usual and prick the base of the pastry with a fork, so that any air trapped underneath can escape rather than cause the pastry to bubble up.

Place a square of non-stick baking paper in the pastry case and, taking care not to damage the edges of the pastry, half-fill the paper with dried beans or ceramic baking beans. Bake as instructed in the recipe, usually for about 10 minutes, then remove the paper and beans. Return the pastry case to the oven for 5–10 minutes, if required to crisp the base.

Pastry Decorations

Making Pastry Leaves

These are a traditional garnish for savoury pies. Pile any pastry trimmings on top of each other in a stack – do not press them into a ball, since they will rise unevenly. Roll out to about 3 mm/⅛ inch thick.

Cut the pastry into long, narrow strips, about 2.5 cm/1 inch wide. Make diagonal cuts across the strips to create diamond shapes. Pressing the knife gently against the pastry, but taking care not to cut right through, mark the veins on each leaf.

Arrange the leaves slightly overlapping on top of the pie, securing them to the crust by brushing underneath with a little water, milk or beaten egg.

Making a Pastry Rose or Tassel

This is a quick decoration for savoury pies. Roll out the pastry to 3 mm/⅛ inch thick and cut a long, broad strip. Make cuts into the pastry at narrow intervals down one long side about two-thirds of the way across the strip. Brush the uncut edge of the strip with water or milk, then roll it up carefully, holding the uncut side. Fan out the cut edge into a tassel.

Making a Pastry Lattice

A lattice of pastry looks attractive on savoury or sweet tarts or pies. Keep the lattice strips apart, leaving wide gaps to show the filling or arrange them almost touching to make a closed lattice top.

Cut the pastry into long, narrow strips. Starting at one side of the tart, overlap the strips, weaving them alternately under and over each other, to make a wide trellis. Attach the strips to the edge of the tart by moistening each one with water and pressing it lightly in place. Then trim off the excess with a knife.

Making Decorative Pastry Edges

Plait

Cut 3 long, narrow strips of pastry. Pinch them together at one end and press this on the rim of the pie. Plait the strips around the pie, joining in extra lengths of pastry as necessary to go all around. Tuck the ends under.

Twist

Cut 2 long, thin strips of pastry and pinch them together at one end. Attach this to the pie rim and then twist the strips gently, arranging around the pie edge as you go.

Shapes

Use small cutters or a sharp knife to cut flowers, fish, leaves or other fancy shapes from pastry trimmings. Moisten the pastry rim and arrange the shapes overlapping around the edge.

Using Filo Pastry

Filo pastry has a reputation for being difficult to handle, but if you follow these simple guidelines, you will find that it is no more difficult to use than other pastry. To keep filo soft and workable, keep the pastry covered when not in use. Lay a sheet of clingfilm over it or keep it wrapped, since the pastry will become brittle and break easily if it dries out.

Work quickly, using up any broken or torn pieces of filo pastry between whole sheets (no-one will notice). Do not moisten filo pastry with water since this will make the sheets stick together and disintegrate (keep the work surface dry for this reason). Use fat to seal edges and to brush the pastry for crisp results.

Choice of Fat

Melted butter is the best choice for flavour, or margarine if you prefer. Low-fat spreads are not suitable for filo because they contain too much water. Olive oil is ideal if the pastry is to be used for savoury dishes, but corn oil or a light oil is a better choice for sweet recipes. Alternatively, mix equal quantities of melted butter and oil.

Making Filo Moneybags or Bundles

1 Cut the pastry into 10 cm/4 inch squares and brush each square with melted butter or oil. Arrange 3–4 filo squares on top of each other, setting each square at a slightly different angle from the one below.
2 Place a spoonful of filling into the centre of the stack of squares.
3 Gather up the points of the pastry over the filling and pinch the pastry around the filling, leaving the pointed edges as a decorative top,

standing slightly apart and outwards. Brush with melted butter or oil. Repeat with the remaining squares and filling. Bake in a hot oven until golden.
4 To garnish savoury moneybags, tie a strip of fresh chive in a tiny bow around the neck of each baked pastry.

Filo Pie Topping

To make a simple filo pie top, scrunch the pastry loosely over the surface of the filling, creating a soft draped-fabric effect. Brush the pastry with a little melted butter, then sprinkle with some sesame seeds or chopped nuts before baking.

Basic Pastry Recipes

Shortcrust Pastry

The classic choice for savoury and sweet everyday dishes, shortcrust pastry is easy to handle and holds its shape well for pies and flan cases.

Makes: **200 g/7 oz**
Preparation time: about 10 minutes

200 g/7 oz plain flour
pinch of salt
100 g/3½ oz fat, such as equal quantities of
   butter and white vegetable fat
2–3 tablespoons iced water

1 Sift the flour and salt into a bowl. Cut the fat into small pieces and add it to the flour.
2 Use your fingertips to rub the fat into the flour very lightly and evenly, until it begins to resemble fine breadcrumbs.
3 Sprinkle the water over the surface and stir with a palette knife until the mixture begins to clump together.
4 Turn out the pastry on to a lightly floured surface and press it together lightly with the fingers. Chill before use.

All-in-One Shortcrust Pastry

This is a great quick-mix recipe for use when you are short of time. The result is pastry which is short and crisp, and useful instead of traditional shortcrust. This recipe makes enough pastry to line a 25 cm/10 inch flan tin.

Makes: **250 g/8 oz**
Preparation time: about 5 minutes

250 g/8 oz plain flour
pinch of salt
140 g/4½ oz soft margarine
2 tablespoons cold water

Place all the ingredients in a bowl. Mix with a fork until the ingredients form a soft, smooth dough. Chill before use.

Basic Pâté Sucrée

A sweet, enriched shortcrust pastry, this has a rich, biscuit-like texture suitable for sweet flans and pastries. This makes enough pastry to line a 20 cm/8 inch flan tin.

Makes: **175 g/6 oz**
Preparation time: about 10 minutes

175 g/6 oz plain flour
pinch of salt
75 g/3 oz unsalted butter, slightly softened
2 egg yolks
1 tablespoon cold water
40 g/1½ oz caster sugar

1 Sift the flour and salt into a pile on to a cold worksurface and make a well in the centre.
2 Add the butter, egg yolks, water and sugar to the well and use the fingertips of one hand to work them together into a rough paste. The mixture should resemble scrambled egg.
3 Gradually work in the flour with your fingertips to bind the mixture into a smooth dough. Press together lightly and form into a ball. Wrap in clingfilm and chill before use.

Suet Pastry

This is a light, spongy pastry for baked or steamed pies and puddings, both savoury and sweet. It can also be used for dumplings.

Makes: **200 g/7 oz**
Preparation time: about 10 minutes

200 g/7 oz self-raising flour
pinch of salt
100 g/3½ oz shredded beef or vegetable suet
about 125 ml/4 fl oz cold water

1 Sift the flour and salt into a bowl, then stir in the suet.
2 Stir in just enough cold water to bind the ingredients into a fairly soft, but not sticky, dough. Press the dough together with your fingertips. Use straight away.

Choux Pastry

As a pastry, this breaks all the rules – it needs lots of heat and firm handling for good results. Use it for sweet or savoury buns, profiteroles, beignets and éclairs.

Makes: **enough for 20 profiteroles**
Preparation time: about 10 minutes

60 g/2¼ oz plain flour
pinch of salt
40 g/1½ oz butter
125 ml/4 fl oz water
2 large eggs, beaten

1 Sift the flour and salt on to a sheet of greaseproof paper.
2 Place the butter and water in a saucepan and heat gently until the butter melts, then bring to

the boil. (Do not bring to the boil before the butter melts.)

3 Draw the pan off the heat and immediately add the flour, all at once. Beat with a wooden spoon or electric hand mixer just until the mixture forms a smooth ball which leaves the sides of the pan clean. Do not overbeat at this stage or the paste will become oily.

4 Cool the mixture for 2 minutes. Gradually add the eggs, beating hard after each addition, and continue to beat until the mixture is smooth and glossy. The paste should be just soft enough to fall gently from the spoon. Use the pastry immediately or cover closely and chill until needed.

Cheat's Rough Puff Pastry

This deliciously rich and crisp, slightly flaky pastry is ideal for single-crust pies, pasties or sweet pastries. It does not rise as much as puff or flaky pastry, but it is far quicker and easier to make! The butter should be chilled until almost frozen, so put it in the freezer 15–20 minutes before you start. It helps if the grater is also chilled.

Makes: **250 g/8 oz**
Preparation time: about 10 minutes

250 g/8 oz plain flour
pinch of salt
175 g/6 oz butter, thoroughly chilled
about 150 ml/¼ pint iced water
2 teaspoons lemon juice

1 Sift the flour and salt into a bowl. Holding the butter with cool fingertips, or by its folded-back wrapper, grate it coarsely into the flour. Work quickly before the butter softens from the heat of your hand.

2 Stir the grated butter into the flour with a palette knife, then sprinkle with just enough iced water to start binding the ingredients into

a dough. Press the dough lightly together with your fingertips.

3 Turn out the dough on to a lightly floured surface and roll it out into an oblong about three times longer than it is wide.

4 Fold the bottom third of the pastry up and the top third down, then press around the sides with a rolling pin to seal the layers together lightly. Chill before use.

Plum and Almond Tart

The crisp, rich texture of pâté sucrée perfectly complements the lightly spiced filling of this summery tart.

Serves: **6–8**

Preparation time: 20 minutes

Cooking time: 1 hour

Oven temperature: 220°C/425°F/Gas Mark 7

1 quantity Pâté Sucrée (see page 228)
1 tablespoon ground almonds
500 g/1 lb dessert plums, halved and stoned
50 g/2 oz soft brown sugar
½ teaspoon ground cinnamon
2 tablespoons blanched flaked almonds
cream, to serve

1 Roll out the pâté sucrée to line a 20 cm/ 8 inch flan tin (see page 225). Bake blind (see page 225) in a preheated oven, 220°C/425°F/Gas Mark 7, for 10 minutes.

2 Sprinkle the ground almonds in the cooked pastry case and arrange the plum halves on top, skin side upwards, overlapping if necessary.

3 Mix together the sugar, cinnamon and flaked almonds and sprinkle over the plums.

4 Return the tart to the oven and bake for 40 minutes. Serve hot or cold with cream.

Courgette, Tomato and Basil Tartlets

A crisp melting pastry case filled with a mixture of vegetables and set in a light custard is one of the classic dishes of any culinary repertoire. Here is a combination of the summer garden's best – baby courgettes, flavoursome tomatoes and sweet basil.

Serves: **4**

Preparation time: 20 minutes

Cooking time: 40–45 minutes

Oven temperature: 200°C/400°F/Gas Mark 6, then 180°C/350°F/Gas Mark 4

1 quantity Shortcrust Pastry (see page 228)
1–2 tablespoons olive oil
1 onion, finely chopped
1 large tomato, skinned, deseeded and chopped
4 basil leaves, finely chopped
8 baby courgettes, cut into wafer thin slices
2 large eggs
150 ml/¼ pint double cream
4 tablespoons grated mature Cheddar cheese
salt and pepper

1 Divide the pastry into quarters and roll out into circles to line four 11 x 1.5 cm/4½ x ¾ inch flan tins (see page 225). Prick the bases gently with a fork. Put on a baking sheet and bake blind (see page 225) in a preheated oven, 200°C/400°F/Gas Mark 6, for 8–10 minutes. Carefully remove the baking beans and non-stick baking paper, then bake for a further 8–10 minutes.

2 While the flan cases are baking, make the filling. Heat the oil in a frying pan. Add the onion and fry over a low heat for 5 minutes until soft but not coloured, then stir in the chopped tomato and basil.

3 Spoon the filling into the cooked flan cases and arrange the courgette slices decoratively on top. Reduce the oven temperature to 180°C/350°F/Gas Mark 4. Beat the eggs and cream together, season to taste with salt and pepper and pour over the filling. Sprinkle with grated Cheddar cheese and bake for 20–25 minutes until just set and golden. Serve warm or cold.

VARIATION • To make one large flan, roll out the pastry into a circle to line a 20 cm/ 8 inch flan tin (see page 225). Bake blind and fill as above, then bake for 25–30 minutes.

Chicken and Mushroom Pie

Serves: **4**

Preparation time: 20 minutes

Cooking time: 35–40 minutes

Oven temperature: 200°C/400°F/Gas Mark 6

2 tablespoons oil
1 onion, chopped
1 garlic clove, crushed
125 g/4 oz mushrooms, sliced, or small whole button mushrooms
1 tablespoon plain flour
300 ml/½ pint Chicken Stock (see page 39)
500 g/1 lb cooked chicken, diced
1 tablespoon chopped parsley
375 g/12 oz puff pastry, thawed in frozen or 1½ quantities of Rough Puff Pastry (see page 229)
salt and pepper

1 Heat the oil in a frying pan. Add the onion and fry over a medium heat, stirring occasionally, until softened. Add the garlic and mushrooms and cook for 2 minutes. Remove the pan from the heat and stir in the flour. Gradually add the stock and stir until thoroughly blended. Return to the heat and bring to the boil, stirring until thickened. Add the cooked chicken and parsley and season to taste with salt and pepper. Mix thoroughly, then transfer to a 1.2 litre/2 pint pie dish.

2 Roll out the pastry to a shape larger than the dish and use to make a single-crust pie (see page 224).

3 Trim, flake and scallop the edges (see page 224), then decorate with pastry leaves made from the trimmings (see page 226) and make a hole in the centre. Brush with beaten egg and bake in a preheated oven, 200°C/400°F/Gas Mark 6, for 30 minutes, until golden.

Cakes and Biscuits

Baking Ingredients

Eggs

For baking, eggs should be used at room temperature, so that they will hold the maximum amount of air and give a good rise to your cakes and bakes. Very cold eggs tend to curdle in creamed mixtures, making the finished cake heavy and tough.

Sugars and Sweeteners

The type depends on the individual recipe. Caster sugar is the most useful for general baking and golden caster is a good choice for adding colour to simple sponges.

Granulated sugar is coarser than caster sugar and it tends to give baked sponges a speckled appearance. You can grind granulated sugar tor just a few seconds in a food processor to make it finer and produce a good substitute for caster sugar.

Soft light and dark brown sugars are coloured and flavoured fine crystal sugars that can be used instead of caster sugar for extra colour. When using brown sugars, break up any small lumps before adding them to mixtures, otherwise they may not mix in evenly.

Dark and light muscovado sugars are natural brown sugars with fine crystals and natural coatings of molasses, giving a distinctive, rich flavour and colour. Although these may be used in most types of baking, the darker ones tend to be sticky because they have more molasses, so these can give cakes a moister, heavier texture.

Demerara sugar has very large crystals that are too coarse for use in creamed mixtures, but it can be used for cakes made by the melting method (see page 240). It also makes an attractive crunchy finish when sprinkled on top of cakes or biscuits.

Icing sugar is the finest-textured sugar. It is used for making smooth icings and meringues, but because of its fine texture, it gives a poor volume to cake mixtures.

Honey and golden syrup can be used instead of part of the sugar in many cakes. These are very good in cakes made by the melting method. When using honey or syrup instead of sugar, it is best to use about a quarter to a third less (by weight), since they are sweeter and give a moister cake result.

Flours

Self-raising and plain white flour are the usual choice, though some recipes may use wholemeal plain or self-raising flours. Self-raising flour has a balanced amount of raising agent already mixed in, making it convenient for many cakes. In some recipes it is necessary to add extra raising agent.

If a recipe calls for self-raising flour and you have only plain, add 2½ teaspoons baking powder to each 250 g/8 oz plain flour. Sift the baking powder and flour together thoroughly to mix them evenly before use.

Fats

Butter and block margarine are the most commonly used fats in baking and they are generally interchangeable. Butter has the better flavour. Bring these hard fats to room temperature before use and, if necessary, beat them with a wooden spoon to soften them slightly, making them easier to mix.

Soft or tub margarines are best for all-in-one methods, since they do not respond well to extensive creaming. Reduced-fat and low-fat spreads cannot be used successfully in standard recipes, since they contain a high

water content. It is best to avoid them except for recipes tested specifically for their use.

Light-flavoured oils, such as sunflower or corn oil, are good in some cakes, especially those made by the melting method (see page 240). Oils are equivalent in fat content to butter, so use oil in a recipe in the same quantity by weight as you would butter.

Dried Fruit

Dried fruit of all kinds are useful storecupboard standbys for cakes and bakes. Make sure you store them in airtight containers and use them up regularly, since they can become too dry and lacking in flavour when old.

Ready-to-eat, semi-dried fruits, such as apricots or figs, are useful because they do not require soaking before use. Smaller fruits, such as currants and sultanas, do not need soaking, but to make them really plump and bring out their fruity flavours to the full, it is worth soaking them for a few hours in fruit juice, sherry, cider or tea before use. Before use, drain off any liquid that has not been absorbed by the fruit, since it could make the mixture too moist.

Nuts

Many cake recipes use chopped or ground nuts for added texture and flavour. Nuts should always be as fresh as possible. Whole nuts keep better than cut nuts, so if you can, grind or chop your own rather than buying them ready prepared. For example, freshly ground almonds prepared in a food processor have a far better, fresher flavour than those available ready ground.

Baking Techniques

There are four basic methods used in baking. If you are familiar with these, you will be able to tackle just about any cake recipe.

Creaming Method

This is the most popular method for making sponges, such as Victoria Sandwich cake. Cream or beat the fat and sugar together, either by hand or with an electric whisk or processor, until pale in colour and fluffy and light in texture. Add the eggs gradually, beating hard after each addition – if they are added too quickly the mixture may curdle and the cake will be heavy in texture. Finally, fold the flour into the creamed mixture, together with any other additions, such as fruit or nuts.

Whisking Method

In all whisked mixtures, the air trapped when whisking expands in the heat of the oven to act as the main raising agent. The simplest mix is a light sponge without added fat. It is the basis for all kinds of cakes, including Swiss roll, and many gâteaux. Whisk the eggs and sugar together in a bowl standing over a saucepan of hot water. Heating the ingredients speeds up the whisking process. The water should not be boiling, but just kept at a low simmer, so that the gentle heat melts the sugar and begins to set the eggs – too high a heat will make the eggs cook into scrambled eggs. When a pale, thick mousse-like mixture is formed, remove the bowl from the heat. The mixture should be thick enough at this stage to hold a clear trail on the surface when the whisk is lifted. Finally, lightly fold in the well-sifted flour.

Melting Method

This is one of the easiest methods for making cakes. It is usually used for moist mixtures, such as gingerbread. Melt the fat and sugar together in a saucepan with the other liquid ingredients, but not the eggs. Keep the heat low to dissolve the ingredients without boiling, which will spoil the flavour. Remove from the heat and cool slightly before stirring in the beaten eggs, followed quickly by the sifted flour and spices. Mix only enough to combine the ingredients evenly. The heat starts to activate the raising agent straight away, so the quicker you put the mixture in the oven, the better it will rise.

Rubbing-in Method

Scones and teabreads are the most common examples of bakes made by this simple method. This usually uses less than half fat to flour. Rub the fat into the dry ingredients with the fingertips or in a food processor as for Shortcrust Pastry (see page 223). Add the eggs and any other liquid ingredients and mix lightly to combine the ingredients evenly.

Choosing the Right Tin

The main rule here is always to use the size of tin recommended in the recipe. You can change a round tin for a square tin, or the opposite way, but remember that – because of its corners – a square tin should be 2.5 cm/1 inch smaller than a round tin. So, if the recipe is for a 23 cm/9 inch round tin, you can use a 20 cm/8 inch square tin instead.

It is worth buying good-quality cake tins. Not only will they last a lifetime, but your cakes will be noticeably better than those cooked in poor-quality tins.

How to Prepare Cake Tins

For most simple cakes, the only preparation that is needed for the tin is greasing by brushing with oil or melted butter over the base and sides. Placing a round piece of non-stick baking paper in the base ensures that the baked goods turn out easily. For richer cakes, which tend to stick or burn at the edges, the whole tin should be lined.

Lining a Round Tin

1 Grease the base and sides of the tin by brushing with melted butter or oil.

2 Cut a long strip of non-stick baking paper slightly longer than the circumference of the tin and about 4 cm/1½ inch deep. Fold over about 1.5 cm/¾ inch along one long edge, then unfold it leaving a crease.

3 Use scissors to snip down the folded edge of the paper up to the fold. Make diagonal cuts, so that the paper can be eased into the tin and overlapped to fit around the curve at the base of the tin.

4 Place the tin on a piece of non-stick baking paper and draw around it to mark the size of the base. Cut out just inside the line to give a round that will fit snugly inside the tin. Place this in the tin to cover the overlapping snipped edge of the side lining paper.

Protecting Cakes during Long Baking

When cooking rich fruit cakes, the long, slow process tends to dry out or overcook the edges of the cake. To prevent this from happening, wrap a double thickness of brown paper or newspaper around the outside of the tin – the paper should be slightly higher than the side of the tin. Tie the paper firmly in place with string.

Flouring Tins

To prepare sandwich tins for cooking whisked sponges, grease by brushing the base and sides with oil or melted butter. Sprinkle a little flour into the tin. Tilt the tin, tapping it lightly to make sure the flour coats the base and sides evenly, then tip out the excess.

How to Test if Cakes are Cooked

The fact that your cake looks golden brown on top is not always a sure sign that it is fully cooked right through. To check a sponge, press the surface lightly with your fingertips – it should feel springy to the touch and spring back without leaving an impression. Whisked sponge cakes should have shrunk slightly away from the side of the tin.

To check a rich fruit cake, lift the tin from the oven and listen closely to the cake – if you can hear the mixture sizzling, it is not fully cooked. Alternatively, insert a metal skewer into the centre of the cake and pull it out immediately. If it comes out clean without mixture on it, the cake is cooked. If there is sticky mixture on the skewer, the middle of the cake is not cooked.

Quick Finishes for Simple Sponge

Icing Sprinkles
Arrange thin strips of paper at random angles or place cut-out paper shapes on top of the sponge. Sift icing sugar from a sieve over the cake, then remove the paper carefully to leave a pattern on the cake.

Lemon Glacé Drizzles
Mix icing sugar with just enough lemon juice to make a runny paste. Place this in a small greaseproof paper piping bag, then cut off the tip and drizzle the icing over the surface of the cake. Scatter with fine strips of lemon rind.

Honeyed Coconut Curls
Brush the surface of the cake with warmed honey, then sprinkle with toasted curls of fresh or dried coconut.

Covering Cakes with Sugarpaste

Ready-to-roll sugarpaste icing is the simplest icing for a cake, for any occasion. You can buy coloured as well as plain white icing. Cover a rich fruit cake with a layer of almond paste first if you plan to store it for longer than a week, otherwise the sugarpaste can be placed directly on the cake.

1 Knead the sugarpaste until it is smooth and pliable. Dust a work surface and rolling pin lightly with cornflour and roll out the sugarpaste to about 5 cm/2 inches larger than the cake.
2 Roll the icing around the rolling pin and gently unroll it over the cake, so that it drapes down the sides.
3 Dust your hands lightly with cornflour and smooth the icing on to the cake, easing it over the sides and pushing out any air bubbles without creasing the icing.
4 Use a sharp knife to trim off the excess icing around the base. Then roll a straight-sided glass jar around the side to smooth the the surface of the icing level and press it firmly against the cake.
5 Use your hands to rub the surface of the

icing until smooth. Decorate with shapes cut from sugarpaste trimmings or with piped icing.

Making a Paper Icing Bag or Cone

1 Cut a 23 cm/9 inch square of greaseproof or non-stick baking paper and fold it in half diagonally to form a triangle.

2 Lift one corner of the folded side and curl it around to the front of the centre point of the triangle.

3 Take the opposite corner of the folded side across to meet the back of the centre point, forming a cone. Fold the points over together firmly or staple them together to hold in place.

4 Snip the very tip from the bag for plain piping, or cut about 5 mm/¼ inch from the end if you want to insert a piping nozzle. With running icing or melted chocolate, it is best to fill the bag before snipping off the tip.

Simple Chocolate Decorations

Chocolate Scrolls or Shavings

Pour some melted chocolate on to a marble slab or the back of a firm baking sheet and spread it out with a palette knife to about 3 mm/⅛ inch thick. Leave until just firm. Use a long, sharp, straight-bladed knife to push across the surface of the chocolate at a 25–45° angle, curling off a thin scroll of chocolate as you go.

Quick Chocolate Curls

Drag a vegetable peeler across a bar of chocolate to make small curls of chocolate.

This works best if the unwrapped bar of chocolate is slightly warmed in your hand.

Chocolate Leaves

Use a small brush to paint an even layer of melted chocolate over the back of clean, dry rose leaves, bay leaves or other non-poisonous leaves. Place on non-stick baking paper and leave to set, then peel off the leaves to leave an imprint of the leaf in the chocolate, ready to decorate special cakes and desserts.

Strawberry Layer Gâteau

This must be the perfect dinner-party dessert – it both looks and tastes wonderful. The sponge layers can be made up to three days in advance and stored in an airtight container.

Makes: **one 22–23 cm/8½–9 inch cake**

Preparation time: 15–20 minutes

Cooking time: 25–30 minutes

Oven temperature: 180°C/350°F/Gas Mark 4

250 g/8 oz butter
250 g/8 oz caster sugar
4 large eggs, beaten
50 g/2 oz ground almonds
150 g/5 oz self-raising flour
Chocolate Curls (see page 243), to decorate
FILLING
250 g/8 oz strawberries
200 ml/7 fl oz double cream, lightly whipped

1 Grease 2 x 22–23 cm/8½–9 inch sandwich tins and line the bases with greaseproof paper (see page 241). Cream the butter and sugar until fluffy and light in colour (see page 240). Gradually beat in the eggs, adding a tablespoon of the ground almonds with the last amount. Sift in the flour and fold it into the mixture with the remaining almonds.

2 Turn into the prepared tins and bake in a preheated oven, 180°C/350°F/Gas Mark 4, for 20–25 minutes, or until the cakes are golden brown. Leave in the tins for 2–3 minutes, then turn out on to a wire rack to cool.

3 Halve or, if they are very large, quarter the strawberries. Reserve a few halves for decoration, with their green tops in place, if liked. Spread three-quarters of the cream on one of the sponges and top with the strawberries. Sandwich the cakes together and spread the remaining cream on the top sponge. Decorate the top with the reserved strawberries and chocolate curls.

Rich Fruit Cake

Long cooking at a low temperature results in a rich, moist cake which is ideal for icing for a special occasion, such as Christmas, a birthday or even a wedding.

Makes: **one 20 cm/8 inch round cake**

Preparation time: 10–15 minutes

Cooking time: 3½ hours

Oven temperature: 160°C/325°F/Gas Mark 3, then 150°C/300°F/Gas Mark 2, then 140°C/275°F/Gas Mark 1

250 g/8 oz butter
250 g/8 oz brown sugar
6 eggs
250 g/8 oz plain flour
1½ teaspoons ground mixed spice
1 tablespoon cocoa powder
grated rind and juice of 2 oranges
grated rind and juice of 1 lemon
250 g/8 oz currants
250 g/8 oz sultanas
250 g/8 oz raisins
175 g/6 oz chopped mixed peel
175 g/6 oz glacé cherries, chopped
50 g/2 oz blanched almonds, chopped
TO COVER
750 g/1½ lb almond paste
slightly warmed, sieved apricot jam

1 Line a deep 20 cm/8 inch round cake tin with greaseproof paper and grease well (see page 241).

2 Cream the butter and sugar together until fluffy and light in colour (see page 240). Beat in the eggs, one at a time. Sift the flour with the spice and cocoa and stir in. Stir in all the remaining ingredients and mix well.

3 Spoon the mixture into the prepared tin and spread evenly. Bake in a preheated oven, 160°C/325°F/Gas Mark 3, for 30 minutes. Reduce the oven temperature to 150°C/300°F/Gas Mark 2 and bake for a further 1 hour. Reduce the oven temperature to 140°C/275°F/Gas Mark 1 and bake for a further 2 hours, or until cooked (see page 242).

4 Turn the cake out to cool on a wire rack.

5 Wrap the cake in greaseproof paper and foil and store for at least 1 month before using.

6 Brush the top and sides of the cake with the jam before covering with the rolled out almond paste.

SUGARPASTE ICING

Makes: **enough to cover a 20 cm/8 inch round cake**

Preparation time: 10 minutes

800 g/1 lb 10 oz icing sugar, plus extra for dusting
2 egg whites
4 tablespoons glucose, warmed
Paste food colours or food colouring, to decorate (optional)

1 Sift the icing sugar into a bowl. Make a well in the centre, add the egg whites and warmed glucose and begin to mix the sugar into the centre with a wooden spoon.

2 Continue mixing until all the sugar has been incorporated.

3 Turn out the icing and knead on a cold work surface dusted with icing sugar until smooth and pliable. Reserve a small portion of the icing for making decorations, if liked. Use the remainder to cover the cake by following the instructions on page 242.

3 Add a dab of paste food colour with the tip of a knife or with a cocktail stick, or a couple of drops of food colouring, to the reserved icing. Knead to incorporate the colour evenly. Roll out the icing and cut out simple shapes, such as flowers or stars, using a template or small cutters. Use to decorate the top of the cake, applying a little egg white to the white icing to stick them in place.

VARIATION • Paste food colours are more concentrated than ordinary liquid food colouring, and offer a wider choice of colours.

Triple Chocolate Muffins

A chocoholic's delight, these muffins are irresistible as soon as they are cool enough to eat.

Makes: **12**

Preparation time: 15 minutes

Cooking time: 25–30 minutes

Oven temperature: 200°C/400°F/Gas Mark 6

300 g/10 oz plain chocolate, chopped
50 g/2 oz unsalted butter, melted
1 egg
350 ml/12 fl oz milk
375 g/12 oz self-raising flour
1 tablespoon baking powder
50 g/2 oz cocoa powder
100 g/3½ oz caster sugar
50 g/2 oz white chocolate buttons

1 Line a 12-cup deep bun tin or muffin tin with paper muffin cases. Melt 175 g/6 oz of the plain chocolate, then stir in the melted butter.

2 Beat together the egg and milk and slowly beat this mixture into the melted chocolate.

3 Sift the flour, baking powder and cocoa powder into a bowl. Stir in the sugar.

4 Add the liquid mixture to the dry ingredients, then the remaining chopped chocolate and the chocolate buttons.

5 Using a large metal spoon, gently fold the ingredients together until just combined. Divide the mixture among the paper cases. Bake in a preheated oven, 200°C/400°F/Gas Mark 6, for 20–25 minutes, until well risen and just firm. Serve the muffins warm or cold.

Butter Shortbread

A light hand is required to ensure that shortbread has a crisp texture and is a melt-in-the mouth treat.

Serves: **8–10**

Preparation time: 15–20 minutes

Cooking time: 30–35 minutes

Oven temperature: 160°C/325°F/Gas Mark 3

125 g/4 oz plain flour
50 g/2 oz cornflour
50 g/2 oz caster sugar
125 g/4 oz butter, plus extra for greasing

1 Sift together the flour and cornflour. Add the sugar and rub in the butter (see page 240). The mixture will become crumbly at first, but continue rubbing in with your fingertips until it clings together in heavy clumps.

2 Turn on to a board or working surface lightly dusted with flour or cornflour and knead lightly. Roll out to a 20 cm/8 inch circle and place on a greased baking sheet. Prick all over the top with a fork, mark into 8 or 10 portions and flute the edges with your fingers.

3 Bake in a preheated oven, 160°C/325°F/Gas Mark 3, for 30–35 minutes, until the shortbread is cooked but not browned. Leave on the baking sheet for 10 minutes, then lift off with a fish slice and place carefully on a wire rack to cool completely. Break into portions to serve.

Index

Acknowledgments

Special Photography: Simon Smith

Other Photography: Octopus Publishing Group Ltd/Sandra Lane/
Ian Wallace/David Loftus/Jean Cazals

Special Photography Home Economists: Lucy Knox and Sarah Lowman